IntelliJ IDEA Essentials

Develop better software fast with IntelliJ IDEA

Jarosław Krochmalski

BIRMINGHAM - MUMBAI

D1456194

IntelliJ IDEA Essentials

First published: December 2014

Production reference: 1161214

Published by Packt Publishing Ltd.
Livery Place
35 Livery Street
Birmingham B3 2PB, UK.

ISBN 978-1-78439-693-0

www.packtpub.com

Credits

Author
Jarosław Krochmalski

Reviewers
Scott Battaglia
Andrew C. Dvorak
Grzegorz Ligas
Jan Thomä

Commissioning Editor
Dipika Gaonkar

Acquisition Editors
Ellen Bishop
Sam Wood

Content Development Editor
Govindan K

Technical Editor
Aman Preet Singh

Copy Editors
Roshni Banerjee
Adithi Shetty

Project Coordinator
Shipra Chawhan

Proofreaders
Simran Bhogal
Stephen Copestake
Maria Gould
Ameesha Green
Paul Hindle

Indexer
Monica Ajmera Mehta

Production Coordinator
Conidon Miranda

Cover Work
Conidon Miranda

About the Author

Jarosław Krochmalski is a passionate software designer and developer who specializes in the financial business domain. He has over 12 years of experience in software development. He is a clean-code and software craftsmanship enthusiast. He is a Certified ScrumMaster and a fan of Agile. His professional interests include new technologies in web application development, design patterns, enterprise architecture, and integration patterns. He likes to experiment with NoSQL and cloud computing.

Jarosław has been working with IDEA since its first release and has observed the IDE grow and mature. He has been designing and developing software professionally since 2000 and has been using Java as his primary programming language since 2002. In the past, he worked for companies such as Kredyt Bank (KBC) and Bank BPS on many large-scale projects such as international money orders, express payments, and collection systems. He currently works as a consultant for the Danish company 7N and writes software for the Nykredit bank. You can reach him via Twitter at @jkroch or by e-mail at jarek@finsys.pl.

I would like to thank my wife, Marylka, and my two boys, Wojtuś and Mati, for being patient and letting me finish the book. Without their help and understanding, this book would not have been possible.

I would like to thank all the people at Packt Publishing, especially Govindan K, Aman Preet Singh, Ellen Bishop, Richard Gall, and Sam Wood—you've made the entire writing and publishing process very smooth and straightforward. A special thanks to all the technical reviewers and proofreaders for providing me with valuable feedback from which I have learned a lot. Thank you.

Greetings to my friends at 7N, Nykredit, Kredyt Bank, and Bank BPS—I hope you enjoy reading the book as much as I enjoyed writing it.

About the Reviewers

Scott Battaglia is a senior software development engineer for Audible Inc. (http://www.audible.com/), which is an Amazon.com, Inc. company and the leading provider of premium digital spoken audio information. He currently leads the shared Android platform team and coaches on a variety of topics, including open source, interviewing, and Scrum. Prior to this, he was an identity management architect and senior application developer with Rutgers, the State University of New Jersey.

He actively contributed to various open source projects, including Apereo Central Authentication Service (CAS) and Inspektr, and has previously contributed to Spring Security, Apereo OpenRegistry, and Apereo uPortal. He has spoken at a variety of conferences, including Jasig, EDUCAUSE, and Spring Forward on topics such as CAS, identity management, Spring Security, and software development practices.

Grzegorz Ligas is a software developer passionate about delivering solutions that are efficient and reliable. He started his career with a small company, writing software for the manufacturing industry, and then moved to retail banking. He currently works for an investment bank in London. Working in various sectors exposed him to technologies varying from mobile to highly distributed grid applications. He's the author of, and main contributor to, the IntelliJ XQuery Support plugin whose goal is to make XQuery development a pleasure.

Jan Thomä is an IT consultant with over 15 years of experience in the IT industry. He has worked for various organizations and businesses, both small and large, including the City of Hamburg, Deutsche Telekom, and the Social Democratic Party of Germany. He has been using and endorsing IntelliJ IDEA ever since he discovered it in 2005 while searching for a truly productive and integrated development environment. He wrote and contributed to several plugins for the IntelliJ platform, including the OSGi and Leiningen plugins.

www.PacktPub.com

Support files, eBooks, discount offers, and more

For support files and downloads related to your book, please visit www.PacktPub.com.

Did you know that Packt offers eBook versions of every book published, with PDF and ePub files available? You can upgrade to the eBook version at www.PacktPub.com and, as a print book customer, you are entitled to a discount on the eBook copy. Get in touch with us at service@packtpub.com for more details.

At www.PacktPub.com, you can also read a collection of free technical articles, sign up for a range of free newsletters, and receive exclusive discounts and offers on Packt books and eBooks.

https://www2.packtpub.com/books/subscription/packtlib

Do you need instant solutions to your IT questions? PacktLib is Packt's online digital book library. Here, you can search, access, and read Packt's entire library of books.

Why subscribe?

- Fully searchable across every book published by Packt
- Copy-and-paste, print, and bookmark content
- On-demand and accessible via a web browser

Free access for Packt account holders

If you have an account with Packt at www.PacktPub.com, you can use this to access PacktLib today and view nine entirely free books. Simply use your login credentials for immediate access.

Table of Contents

Preface   **1**

Chapter 1: Get to Know Your IDE, Fast   **7**

Comparing the various editions   **7**
Installing IntelliJ IDEA   **8**
An overview of the workspace   **9**
  Tool windows   9
  View modes in tool windows   11
    Pinned Mode   11
    Docked Mode   11
    Floating Mode   12
    Split Mode   12
  Multiple views in tool windows   13
    Navigating inside the tool window   14
    Tool windows set up for a specific project   15
  Editor tabs   16
Crafting your settings   **17**
  Searching for options   17
  Setting keyboard shortcuts   17
  Colors and fonts   18
  Picking your plugins   19
Configuration tips and tricks   **21**
  Exporting and importing settings   21
  Sharing settings   22
  Tuning IntelliJ IDEA   23
Summary   **24**

Chapter 2: Off We Go – To the Code   25

What is a project?   26
Project structure and configuration   26
Comparison of Eclipse, NetBeans, and IntelliJ IDEA terminologies   27
The project   27
Modules   28
Folders   29
Libraries   31
Facets   33
Artifacts   35

Creating a project   37
Creating a new project from scratch   38
Importing the existing project   40
Project format   43
The directory-based format   44
The file-based format   44
The directory-based format versus the file-based format   45

Summary   45

Chapter 3: The Editor   47

An overview of the editor and setup   47
The gutter area   48
The Status bar   51
Tabs   53
Scratches   55
Scrollbar   56

Navigating in the editor   57
Navigating between files   58
Navigating within a single file   64
The Search Everywhere feature   66

The editor basics   67
Searching for and replacing text   67
Syntax-aware selection   69
Column selection mode   69
Clipboard history   70
Reformatting the code   70
Code completion   71
Language injection   73
Generating code   74
Code inspection   75

Using Live Templates   76
Postfix code completion   79

Comparing files and folders — **80**
  Comparing files — 80
  Comparing folders — 82
Looking for help — **83**
  Viewing inline documentation — 84
  Viewing type definitions — 84
  Looking for usages — 85
  Viewing method parameters — 85
  Viewing the external documentation — 86
Summary — **87**
Chapter 4: Make It Better – Refactoring — **89**
  An overview of refactoring — **89**
  Refactoring actions — **95**
    Rename — 95
    Find and Replace Code Duplicates — 96
    Copy — 96
    Move — 97
    Move Instance Method — 99
    Safe Delete — 99
    Change Signature — 100
    Type Migration — 101
    Make Static — 101
    Convert to Instance Method — 101
    Extract refactorings — 102
    Extract Variable — 102
    Extract Constant — 102
    Extract Field — 103
    Extract Parameter — 104
    Introduce Parameter Object — 105
    Extract Method — 105
    The Extract Method object — 106
    Delegate — 107
    Extract Interface — 109
    Extract Superclass — 110
    Inline — 110
    Remove Middleman — 112
    Wrap Return Value — 112
    Invert Boolean — 113
    Pull Members Up or Push Members Down — 113
    Replace Inheritance With Delegation — 113

Convert Anonymous Class to Inner	114
Encapsulate Fields	115
Replace Constructor with Factory Method / Builder	116
Generify	116
Summary	**118**
Chapter 5: Make It Happen – Running Your Project	**119**
A temporary configuration	**120**
The permanent configuration	**121**
The Run/Debug configuration for a Java application	122
Creating a Tomcat server local configuration	128
The Node.js configuration	133
Configuration defaults	**134**
Sharing the configuration	**135**
Running	**136**
Summary	**138**
Chapter 6: Building Your Project	**139**
Editing Maven settings	**140**
The Maven tool window	**144**
Running Maven goals	**144**
Using Gradle	**148**
Executing Gradle tasks	**150**
Summary	**151**
Chapter 7: Red or Green? Test Your Code	**153**
Enabling the testing plugins	**154**
Creating the test	**156**
Creating a run/debug configuration for the test	**160**
Running or debugging the test	**164**
Keyboard shortcuts	**170**
Summary	**170**
Chapter 8: Squash'em – The Debugger	**171**
Debugger settings	**171**
Setting up the JavaScript debugger	**178**
Managing breakpoints	**180**
Starting the debugger	**191**
The Debug tool window	**193**
Inspecting variables and evaluating expressions	**196**
Debugger actions	**203**
Keyboard shortcuts summary	**206**
Summary	**206**

Chapter 9: Working with Your Team   207
Enabling version control   207
Configuring version control   210
Working with version control   217
Changelists   217
Adding files to version control   218
Committing files   220
Getting changes from the repository   224
Browsing the changes   226
Reverting the local changes   227
Using the difference viewer   228
Displaying the history   231
The log viewer   233
Quickly executing VCS actions   234
Keyboard shortcuts   236
Summary   236
Chapter 10: Not Enough? Extend It   237
Setting up the environment and project   238
Developing the plugin functionality   241
Deploying and publishing   247
Summary   251
Index   253

Preface

The first version of IntelliJ IDEA was released in January 2001. It is a mature, integrated development environment (IDE), designed to help you in the coding process, and supports a large number of different frameworks, tools, and targets. It works with multiple programming languages. It now includes full support for Java 8 and Java EE 7.

The key objective of IntelliJ IDEA is to increase and assist developer productivity. Whether you develop in Java, Scala, or PHP, or make the frontend using HTML and JavaScript, IntelliJ IDEA's smart and relevant suggestions and code completion, on-the-fly code analysis, and respectable refactoring tools will support you in every step.

When you are migrating from NetBeans or Eclipse, you will quickly see that IntelliJ IDEA is different because it *understands the context*. The IDE knows where you are in the editor and reacts accordingly; you will be surprised at how smart IntelliJ IDEA behaves.

This tool is a generic workhorse rather than a strict Java IDE. In this book, you will learn how to make IntelliJ IDEA work for you and get your job done in the most efficient and pleasant way.

What this books covers

Although the book describes the latest version of IntelliJ IDEA - 14, most of the concepts will also work on the previous revision of the IDE.

Chapter 1, *Get to Know Your IDE, Fast*, is a very concise note on editions comparison, requirements and installing IntelliJ IDEA in Windows, OSX, and Linux. This chapter guides you through the main workspace and show you ways to customize it for different tasks, presenting briefly the most useful plugins, IDE settings, and configuration tips.

Chapter 2, Off We Go – To the Code, describes the process of setting up a new project or importing an existing one. The chapter explains terminology differences with NetBeans and Eclipse and presents the concept of modules and artifacts.

Chapter 3, The Editor, describes the core of IntelliJ IDEA – the editor. In this chapter, you use state-of-the-art code completion, templates, and other great IntelliJ IDEA features. This chapter shows how to set up the editor and gives you some productivity tips.

Chapter 4, Make It Better – Refactoring, presents the powerful refactoring toolset of IntelliJ IDEA. You are guided through the most useful refactoring techniques.

Chapter 5, Make It Happen – Running Your Project, covers configuring the runtime environment for your project. We also talk about adding run configurations, either on the server or standalone. This chapter focusses not only on Java, but on other technologies such as Node.js as well.

Chapter 6, Building Your Project, focusses on building a project. You use IntelliJ IDEA's own build system, and Maven and Gradle integration as well.

Chapter 7, Red or Green? Test Your Code, is all about unit testing in IntelliJ IDEA. We focus on setting IntelliJ IDEA up specifically to run tests. You create JUnit and TestNG run configurations and then run and debug the tests. Then, you are given a brief overview of the test runner windows, useful settings, and option suggestions.

Chapter 8, Squash'em – The Debugger, focusses on the IntelliJ IDEA debugger. You get familiar with the debugger tool window and debugger options. We look under the hood – evaluating expressions, using watches, conditional breakpoints, and other debugger features. We also talk briefly about remote debugging.

Chapter 9, Working with Your Team, This chapter is all about version control, and managing change lists and tasks. There is a brief description on how to set up VCS integration, with the main focus on Git. This chapter describes integration with popular bug trackers, such as JIRA and YouTRACK.

Chapter 10, Not Enough? Extend It, describes briefly the plugin architecture of IntelliJ IDEA. We talk about possibilities and develop a simple plugin, so that you have knowledge of how to extend the IDE. You are also presented with useful links and resources to develop your knowledge even further.

What you need for this book

You will need a Mac or PC, running OS X, MS Windows, or Linux, to be able to set up and run IntelliJ IDEA. To learn the presented features, you will also need the tool itself, of course. You can use the free 30-day trial of Ultimate Edition or use the Community Edition, which is available free of charge. We will flag the differences and let you know what features are not available in the free version of the IDE. You can read how to get it in *Chapter 1, Get to Know Your IDE, Fast*.

Who this book is for

This book is a fast-paced introduction to IntelliJ IDEA and is aimed at users who want to learn the essentials of the new IDE in a nimble and efficient way.

Conventions

In this book, you will find a number of text styles that distinguish between different kinds of information. Here are some examples of these styles and an explanation of their meaning.

Code words in text, database table names, folder names, filenames, file extensions, pathnames, dummy URLs, user input, and Twitter handles are shown as follows: "If you keep getting OutOfMemoryError in PermGen space exceptions, try to change the -XX:MaxPermSize setting."

A block of code is set as follows:

```
private boolean isValid(int a) {
  return a > 15 && a < 100;
}
```

Any command-line input or output is written as follows:

```
git clone git://git.jetbrains.org/idea/community.git idea
```

New terms and **important words** are shown in bold. Words that you see on the screen, for example, in menus or dialog boxes, appear in the text like this: "To do this, first download the IntelliJ Configuration Server plugin, using the Plugins page of the **Settings** dialog box."

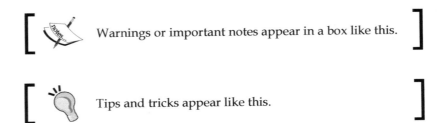

Warnings or important notes appear in a box like this.

Tips and tricks appear like this.

Reader feedback

Feedback from our readers is always welcome. Let us know what you think about this book—what you liked or disliked. Reader feedback is important for us as it helps us develop titles that you will really get the most out of.

To send us general feedback, simply e-mail feedback@packtpub.com, and mention the book's title in the subject of your message.

If there is a topic that you have expertise in and you are interested in either writing or contributing to a book, see our author guide at www.packtpub.com/authors.

Customer support

Now that you are the proud owner of a Packt book, we have a number of things to help you to get the most from your purchase.

Errata

Although we have taken every care to ensure the accuracy of our content, mistakes do happen. If you find a mistake in one of our books—maybe a mistake in the text or the code—we would be grateful if you could report this to us. By doing so, you can save other readers from frustration and help us improve subsequent versions of this book. If you find any errata, please report them by visiting http://www.packtpub. com/submit-errata, selecting your book, clicking on the **Errata Submission Form** link, and entering the details of your errata. Once your errata are verified, your submission will be accepted and the errata will be uploaded to our website or added to any list of existing errata under the Errata section of that title.

To view the previously submitted errata, go to https://www.packtpub.com/books/ content/support and enter the name of the book in the search field. The required information will appear under the **Errata** section.

Piracy

Piracy of copyrighted material on the Internet is an ongoing problem across all media. At Packt, we take the protection of our copyright and licenses very seriously. If you come across any illegal copies of our works in any form on the Internet, please provide us with the location address or website name immediately so that we can pursue a remedy.

Please contact us at `copyright@packtpub.com` with a link to the suspected pirated material.

We appreciate your help in protecting our authors and our ability to bring you valuable content.

Questions

If you have a problem with any aspect of this book, you can contact us at `questions@packtpub.com`, and we will do our best to address the problem.

Get to Know Your IDE, Fast

1

In this chapter, we will compare IntelliJ IDEA editions and licenses, install the tool, and quickly introduce the main workspace. IntelliJ IDEA comes with many settings; it is not possible to cover all of them in one book so we will focus on the most important ones. We will cover the following topics in this chapter:

- Comparing the various editions
- Installing the tool
- Workspace overview
- IDE settings
- Configuration tips and tricks

Comparing the various editions

IntelliJ IDEA is available as a free Community Edition and full-fledged Ultimate Edition. From the licensing point of view, the good thing is you can use both editions to develop the software you want to sell. It is worth mentioning that the new Android Studio that is used for the development of mobile Android applications is also based on IntelliJ IDEA.

The detailed comparison table can be found on the JetBrains website: `http://www.jetbrains.com/idea/features/editions_comparison_matrix.html`. To cut a long story short, there are many features missing in the Community Edition, but there are some workarounds available if you look close enough. For example, when you want to use Tomcat or Jetty servers in the Community Edition, you can use Maven plugins to run and debug your web applications freely. We will discuss this in *Chapter 5, Make It Happen – Running Your Project*.

You can use the Community Edition to develop applications using many frameworks such as Play, Struts, or Spring. It's all Java, after all. The IDE will not assist you in that. Most of the configuration hints, warnings, autocompletion, and runtime configuration features will be unavailable.

The Ultimate Edition, on the other hand, is the full-featured commercial IDE. You have the full support of almost all of the modern frameworks and application servers. The IDE will assist you by providing code completion, hints, and diagrams. The language support in this edition is also more comprehensive; you will get HTML and scripting languages analysis available on the fly, for example.

Apart from the provided features, the Ultimate Edition can be categorized based on the license. Depending on your needs, you can purchase any of the following licenses:

- **Commercial license**: IntelliJ IDEA can be used by any developer in your company but the total number of concurrent users cannot exceed the number of purchased licenses.

- **Personal license**: IntelliJ IDEA can be used only by the person who purchased it. You can use it on as many computers as you own, as long as you are the only user. The Personal license, of course, can also be used to develop commercial products.

Additionally, there are some licensing options and discounts based on the target audience, for startups, students, and teachers, for education or training, and finally, for open source projects.

 When you decide to buy the Ultimate Edition, sometimes it is wise to wait till the holidays, for example, Christmas or Easter. The JetBrains team usually provides some discounts on their products then.

Installing IntelliJ IDEA

Installing IntelliJ IDEA is straightforward. Perform the following steps:

1. Go to `http://www.jetbrains.com/idea/download/`.
2. Pick the OS version and edition of your choice.

3. After opening the downloaded installation package in MS Windows, you should see the installation wizard. In Mac OS, double-click on the downloaded .dmg file and then just drag IntelliJ IDEA to the Applications folder.

 When you install IntelliJ IDEA over an existing installation, the installation wizard will ask if you want to import settings from the previous set up. Don't worry, your settings will be preserved.

During the first startup, IntelliJ IDEA will ask you which plugins should be enabled by default. Usually, it's best to enable only what you need, so the IDE loads and works faster with fewer plugins enabled. Don't worry if you don't know what to select; you can always change your mind later by editing the IDE settings. On the first startup, you will not be able to see the workspace without the project opened. While we will go through the details of creating the project in the next chapter, you can now just create the basic Java project by choosing **New Project** from the **File** menu, selecting **Java**, and proceeding with the **New Project** wizard by clicking on **Next** a couple of times.

An overview of the workspace

Basically, the workspace in IntelliJ IDEA consists of the main editor with tabs, menus, and many tool windows.

Tool windows

The tool windows are hidden, by default, in Version 13 and later of IDEA. You can toggle them on and off using the button in the bottom-left corner of the screen:

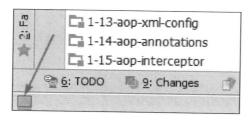

Tool windows are those little "tabs" visible at the edges of the workspace. These edges are called tool window bars, as shown in the following screenshot:

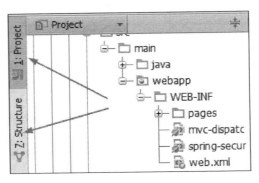

Some of the tool windows are always available, such as **Project** or **Structure**, while some of them are available only when the corresponding plugins are enabled.

You can arrange the order of the tool windows by dragging them with your mouse. You can drag the tool window to other screen edges as well.

There's a fourth tool window bar available at the top of the screen, which is hidden. Just drag any tool window to the top of your workspace to use it, as shown in the following screenshot:

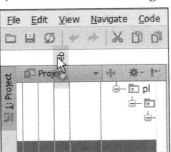

View modes in tool windows

The tool windows have a context menu available when you right-click on them. The context menu contains items specific to a particular tool window and some possible view modes, as shown in the following screenshot:

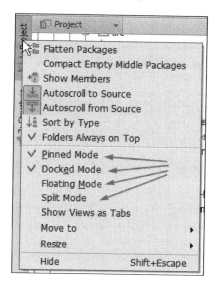

Pinned Mode

The pinned tool window will stay open even when it becomes inactive by losing focus. You may prefer to have the **Project** tool window pinned to have a constant overview of the project structure. Only docked windows can be pinned. On the other hand, you can keep the project view closed almost all the time and simply use the keyboard shortcuts to navigate. On large projects, this approach is much faster than searching the tree manually for your file.

Docked Mode

When docked, the tool window will share the total workspace area with other workspace elements such as the editor. On the other hand, when undocked, the tool window will overlap the other workspace elements when resized. An undocked window will go away if inactive. For example, it is especially useful to have the console tool window undocked and resized; reading huge logfiles or console output will be a lot easier.

Floating Mode

Floating, as the name suggests, allows the tool window to float over the workspace and be detached from the screen edges. It may be useful when you work on multimonitor environments with huge display resolutions set. There are no limiting factors for the number of floating windows shown simultaneously. When floating, tool windows can be easily arranged to suit your needs.

Split Mode

The tool window will share the tool window bar with other tool windows when it has **Split Mode** enabled. This gives you the ability to see two tool windows at once. It's nice to see the project structure and file structure at the same time, as shown in the following screenshot:

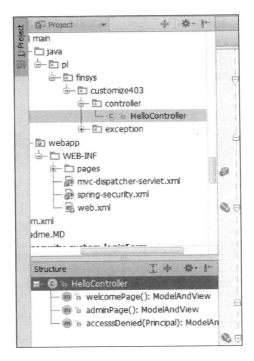

When you use the *Ctrl* + left-click (PC) or *cmd* + left-click (Mac) keyboard shortcuts, the splitter between the two tool windows is displayed at once; IntelliJ IDEA will switch them to the wide screen mode and display them in a horizontal layout. It is priceless when you work on a fancy panoramic display and would like to use the screen space effectively, as shown in the following screenshot:

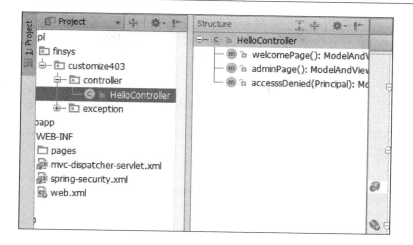

 You can quickly go to the specific tool window by using the mnemonic shortcut displayed before its name, for example, *Alt + 1* (PC) or *cmd + 1* (MAC) will take you to the **Project** tool window. It works for hidden tool windows, too.

Multiple views in tool windows

Some tool windows have more than one view available. For example, the **Project** tool window can show **Project**, **Packages**, or **Problems**, as shown in the following screenshot:

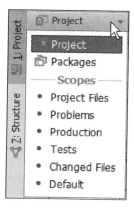

These views can be made visible as separate tabs by selecting **Show views as tabs** in the tool window context menu:

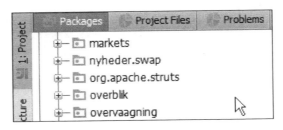

When you have your tool windows set up, it may be a good idea to back up your current layout. You can save the way the tool windows are currently arranged by navigating to **Window | Store Current Layout as Default** in the main menu. You can always load the saved workspace layout by navigating to **Window | Restore Default Layout** or pressing *Shift + F12*.

You can quickly open your last active tool window by using the *F12* (PC) or *Fn + F12* (Mac) keyboard shortcut. To make this shortcut work on Mac, you first need to adjust the *F12* system shortcut behavior in the System Preferences window available in the Apple menu. To quickly hide/unhide all tool windows and focus on the editor, press *Ctrl + Shift+ F12* (PC) or *cmd + Fn + Shift + F12* (Mac).

 The *Esc* key will always get you back into the editor.

When switched off, you can temporarily show the tool window bars by pressing the left *Alt* key (PC) twice or tapping and holding down the left *cmd* button (Mac). This way, you can switch tool windows swiftly and save screen space at the same time.

Navigating inside the tool window

If the tool window contains a list (and most of them do, actually) to navigate or search inside the tool window, focus on the tool window, and just start typing the search text. It doesn't matter if it is a project or another tool window: IntelliJ IDEA will search for the characters you typed on the fly, as shown in the following screenshot:

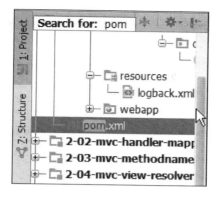

Tool windows set up for a specific project

There is a very useful plugin you can find in the IntelliJ IDEA plugin repository named ToolWindow manager. We will talk more about installing plugins later in this chapter.

This plugin makes tool window buttons available to be controlled on a per-project basis. It allows the creation of tool window profiles, that is, you can set specific tool windows to be hidden for one project and shown for another. This is the way to keep your IDE clean and tidy.

To access the settings, go to **Window | Tool Window Management | Configure Preferred Availabilities** from the main menu, as shown in the following screenshot:

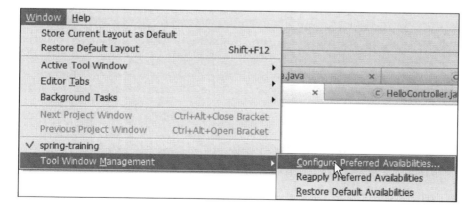

Next, set up preferences for particular tool windows. Select **Hide** to switch off the specific tool window and **Show** to turn it on, as shown in the following screenshot:

Editor tabs

An important part of the workspace is the editor tabs. They represent opened files and have a context menu with file-specific options, such as adding a file to a favorites list or using version control on the file.

Tabs are great to switch files, but there is a drawback here. They occupy some of the editor space when you have many files opened. The limit of the visible tab count can be set by navigating to **Settings | Editor | General | Editor tabs** (PC) or **IntelliJ IDEA | Preferences | Editor | Editor tabs** (Mac) dialog box. IntelliJ IDEA autocloses tabs if the tab count exceeds the defined limit. This is a very useful feature to reduce the tab clutter. IntelliJ IDEA will always close the least used tab.

Consider switching tabs off completely. It may sound a little weird at the beginning, but when you develop the habit of using keyboard shortcuts to navigate through opened files, you will not need tabs, and will regain some of the valuable editor space.

 Use *Ctrl* + *E* (PC) or *cmd* + *E* (Mac) to display the list of opened files. Use *Ctrl* + *Shift* + *E* (PC) or *cmd* + *Shift* + *E* (Mac) to display the list of recently edited files. You can also switch between the last opened files with *Ctrl* + *Tab* and *Ctrl* + *Shift* + *Tab*.

Crafting your settings

In the next section, we will discuss the options of the IDE—setting keyboard shortcuts, colors, fonts, and plugins.

Searching for options

The settings dialog is available from the main menu by navigating to **File | Settings** (PC) or **IntelliJ IDEA | Preferences** (Mac). You can also use the wrench icon on the toolbar or *Ctrl + Alt + S* (PC) or *cmd + ,* (Mac) keyboard shortcuts. All of the settings are divided into two groups: one for project-specific settings (such as code style, version control, and so on) and one for global, IDE settings (such as appearance or HTTP proxy, for example).

There are many options here. The good thing is you can use the search field to search for a specific option. Just start typing the option name and the dialog box will be searched from top to bottom to present you the result.

For example, if you introduce a "typo" in the search box, you will be presented with the **Inspection** project settings, where you can turn the **Spelling/Typo** inspection option off. In the **Editor/Colors & Font/General** section, you can change colors for misspelled words.

Setting keyboard shortcuts

IntelliJ IDEA is a keyboard-centric IDE. Any action you can do by using your mouse, you can do by using the keyboard as well.

It's possible to completely redefine default IntelliJ IDEA keymaps to suit your needs. The keyboard shortcuts configuration is available in the **Keymap** section in the IDE settings.

There are some predefined keymaps available. Whether you come from using Eclipse or NetBeans, you can find your well-known keymap here and apply it. Please note that predefined keymaps are not editable. To modify the keymap, you must create and edit a copy.

When defining a new keyboard shortcut, the **Second Stroke** keyboard shortcut editor feature is very useful. You can use this to set up double strokes, easy to remember keyboard shortcuts, or even shortcut groups. You can define your base shortcut, such as *Ctrl + Shift + O* for example, and then numbers as second strokes, as shown in the following screenshot:

The **Abbreviation** option in the keyboard shortcut editor is used to quickly find the **Search Everything** (double *Shift*) dialog box. The **Search Everything** dialog box will be discussed in *Chapter 3, The Editor*.

Colors and fonts

In IntelliJ IDEA, you can change your preferable colors and font's layout for syntax and error highlighting in the editor, search results, debugger, and consoles.

To do this, open **Editor** and then **Colors & Fonts** in the IDE settings dialog box.

IntelliJ IDEA comes with some predefined color schemes. You can select one of them, or create your own, and configure its settings to your liking.

Note that you are not allowed to change any of the predefined schemes. If you decide to tweak the existing theme, you have to copy it first. To change the editor font, select **Font** from the **Colors & Fonts** section of the IDE settings page.

Many nice color themes can be found at
http://www.ideacolorthemes.org.

For example, if you use the Darcula IDE theme, the Obsidian color scheme looks good, as shown in the following screenshot:

```java
public class Demo {
    private static final String CONSTANT = "String";
    private Object o;
    /**
     * Creates a new demo.
     * @param o The object to demonstrate.
     */
    public Demo(Object o) {
        this.o = o;
        String s = CONSTANT + "Other";
        int i = 123;
    }
    public static void main(String[] args) {
        Demo demo = new Demo();
    }
}
```

 There is a truly great font designed especially for developers: Source Code Pro. This font family was created specifically for coding environments— it's very readable. It's available free of charge from Adobe, at GitHub https://github.com/adobe/source-code-pro.

You can download Source Code Pro for Windows, Linux, and OS X as well.

Picking your plugins

The IntelliJ IDEA plugin repository is available on the Internet at http://plugins.jetbrains.com/?idea or from the IDE itself, by going to the **Plugins** section in the **Settings** page. Going to the **Plugins** section in the IDE is more convenient in comparison to the Internet repository. All you have to do is find your plugin, install, and restart the IDE.

To install JetBrains' plugin, click on the **Install JetBrains plugin...** button. To install a third-party plugin, choose **Browse repositories**. In the next dialog box, you can filter the available plugins by category, or find a specific plugin just by typing its name.

You can sort the list of plugins by the download count or rating to see the most popular (and probably the most useful) plugins at the top of the list:

To deactivate the installed plugin, uncheck the checkbox next to its name. To uninstall the plugin, use the context menu, but take note that bundled JetBrains plugins cannot be uninstalled from within the IDE, as shown here:

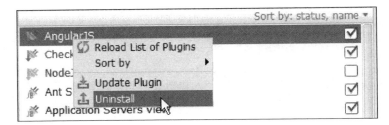

Some of the plugins add new languages to the IntelliJ IDEA arsenal. If you develop in a language other than Java, just filter the plugins list using the **Custom Languages** option. When you install the plugins, the on-the-fly analysis, hints, and refactoring will be available in your IDE. These plugins include, for example, Scala, Python, Ruby, PHP, and many others.

The next huge group of plugins is available when you filter using **Framework Integration**. There is a big chance you will find support for the framework you use in your project, such as AngularJS or Play, for example.

If you are new to IntelliJ IDEA, there is a plugin that is especially useful called Key promoter. It will show you a banner with the keyboard shortcut for the action you just performed using the mouse. It will help you memorize keyboard shortcuts and quickly become a keyboard ninja:

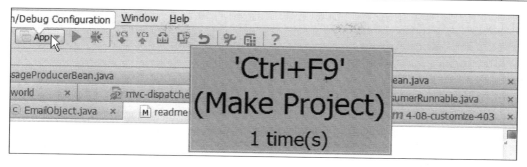

Use the Key promoter plugin available in the plugins repository to see how easy you can make the same action you just did using your mouse, by only using your keyboard!

Feel free to browse JetBrains and the third-party plugins directory. It's a real gold mine to extend the IDE functionality. Select the plugin, read the description to the right, click on **Install**, restart the IDE, and you're all set.

Configuration tips and tricks

In this section, you will be presented with some configuration tips, such as sharing settings and tuning IntelliJ IDEA.

Exporting and importing settings

If you have your IDE set the way you like, it may be a good idea to back up all settings. Sometimes, it's good to have common settings across all team members. IntelliJ IDEA gives you the ability to archive and export all or specific settings.

To export IDE settings to a JAR archive, do the following:

1. Go to **File | Export Settings** from the main menu.

2. Specify the settings to export the **Export Settings** dialog box by selecting the checkboxes next to them. All of them are selected by default.

3. Specify the fully qualified name and path or click on the **Browse** button to choose the target file.

To import IDE settings from a JAR archive, do the following:

1. Go to **File | Import Settings** from the main menu.
2. Select the desired archive from the **Import File Location** dialog box.
3. Specify the settings to be imported in the **Select Components to Import** dialog box and click on **OK**.

You should be really careful with importing settings. Importing a set of settings will overwrite all your settings with the imported set. For example, if you export some live templates and reimport them during a colleague's installation, the import will overwrite all their live templates with the imported ones.

There are many nice-looking themes exported this way, available to be downloaded at http://ideacolorthemes.org. Just pick and import the JAR file and check out how beautiful your IDE will look!

Sharing settings

Sometimes it's good to have the same configuration across all members of your team, organization, or the company. For this purpose, IntelliJ IDEA can use a server to store IDE settings and share them within your team.

To do this, first download the IntelliJ Configuration Server plugin, using the **Plugins** page of the **Settings** dialog box.

To connect to the *IntelliJ Configuration Server*, use your JetBrains account. If you don't have the account, you can create one on the JetBrains website using the link provided in the login dialog.

You can connect to IntelliJ Configuration Server in two ways: during the first startup or on demand.

During the *first* IntelliJ IDEA startup after installing the plugin, you can select the connection option for the next startup, such as **Show login dialog, Login silently,** or **Do not login**.

When the configuration server is connected, the green icon is displayed in the status bar, as shown in the following screenshot:

Otherwise, the red icon will be presented:

You can log in to the *IntelliJ Configuration Server* at any time using the button on the status bar.

The IntelliJ IDEA server stores almost all of the IDE and project settings except for those containing local paths. Your code style settings, keymaps, fonts, color schemes, and inspection profiles will be synced.

Take note that the IntelliJ IDEA server is a public, third-party server. It's secured by a username and password and uses SSL communication, but if you are very concerned about your privacy, you should share your settings using the export/import feature rather than the IntelliJ Configuration Server.

> If you have to use a proxy to access the Internet in your environment, you can set up the proxy settings in the login dialog box.

Tuning IntelliJ IDEA

IDEA's Virtual Machine settings are usually very good out of the box. However, when you work on a specific huge project and decide that you want to tweak IntelliJ IDEA's own virtual machine settings, you can change that in the following locations, depending on your operating system.

On Windows, you can tweak IntelliJ IDEA's own virtual machine settings by executing the following code:

```
<IntelliJ IDEA installation folder>/bin/idea.exe.vmoptions
```

Alternatively, you can use the following code:

```
<IntelliJ IDEA installation folder>/bin/idea64.exe.vmoptions
```

On Linux and Unix systems, you can tweak IntelliJ IDEA's own virtual machine settings by executing the following code:

```
<IntelliJ IDEA installation folder>/bin/idea.vmoptions
```

Alternatively, you can use the following code:

```
<IntelliJ IDEA installation folder>/bin/idea64.vmoptions
```

On OS X, since Version 12, the file `/Applications/IntelliJ IDEA.app/Contents/bin/idea.vmoptions` should be copied to the following path:

```
~/Library/Preferences/IntelliJIdeaXX/idea.vmoptions
```

In this file, you can find, or change, Java Virtual Machine settings that IntelliJ IDEA runs on. For example, to increase the IntelliJ IDEA heap size, modify the `-Xmx` setting. If you keep getting an `OutOfMemoryError` message in the `PermGen space` exceptions, try changing the `-XX:MaxPermSize` setting.

> The file-scanning applications (such as Spotlight or Alfred on OS X, for example) can slow down the IDE a bit; think about excluding IDEA's folders from their scope.
>
> Having an SSD drive to develop helps a lot with the performance. Indexing, looking for usages, and other file-related tasks will be a lot faster on the SSD drive.

Summary

In this chapter, we discussed what IntelliJ IDEA is, briefly presented a comparison of the available editions, and revealed the main workspace elements and how to customize them.

Install IntelliJ IDEA and try to set up your IDE the way you like it. Use the tips provided to configure the workspace like a pro. Back up your configuration or share it with others.

In the next chapter, we will create and import a project and start the actual work.

Off We Go – To the Code

2

This chapter is all about setting up or importing your project in the IDE. We will focus on understanding IntelliJ IDEA concepts such as modules, libraries, and artifacts. We will discuss the difference in terminology and see how the terminology used in IntelliJ IDEA is different from that used in NetBeans and Eclipse, so you can switch from them faster.

We will cover the following topics in this chapter:

- A comparison of Eclipse, NetBeans, and IntelliJ IDEA terminologies
- Project structure and configuration—modules, libraries, facets, and artifacts
- Creating a new project from scratch
- Importing the existing project
- The project's format

What is a project?

Almost everything you do in the IDE is contained within the scope of a project. The project represents the software you are working on—it is the top-level container for all your modules, libraries, and configuration settings. There can be only one project open in a single IDE window. If you would like to have multiple projects open, IntelliJ IDEA will open them in separate, isolated windows. You can switch between the windows using the **Next Project Window** or **Previous Project Window** options from the **Window** menu or using the keyboard shortcut, *Ctrl + Alt +* open/close bracket.

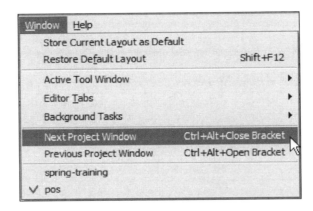

IntelliJ IDEA stores the project's configuration in two different formats. The project's format is covered later in the *Project format* section.

Project structure and configuration

Before we create a new project from scratch or import an existing one, we will focus on IntelliJ IDEA's key concepts that will define the project. We will start by listing the terminology differences between different IDEs and then explain all of the concepts.

Comparison of Eclipse, NetBeans, and IntelliJ IDEA terminologies

IntelliJ IDEA has a different terminology when compared to the terminologies used in Eclipse and NetBeans. The following table compares the Eclipse and IntelliJ IDEA terminologies:

Eclipse	IntelliJ IDEA
Workspace (contains one or more projects)	Project
Project	Module
Project-specific JRE	Module SDK
User library	Global library
Classpath variable	Path variable
Project dependency	Module dependency
Library	Module library

The next table will highlight the differences in the terminology used in NetBeans and IntelliJ IDEA:

NetBeans	IntelliJ IDEA
Project	Module
Project-specific JDK	Module SDK
Global library	Global library
Project library	Module library
Project dependency	Module dependency

Now that we have seen the differences, let's have a closer look at these concepts.

The project

The project is the concept that represents a complete software application. It doesn't contain the source code and other development files such as the build or configuration scripts. It defines the project-wide settings and contains the collection of modules and libraries.

Modules

A project in IntelliJ IDEA consists of modules. A module is a discrete, separate entity that can be compiled, run, and debug autonomously from other modules in the project. The module can contain source code, resources, scripts, documentation, or other files.

At any time, you can import, add, or remove the module from the project using the **Project Structure** dialog box, by navigating to **File | Project structure**. To create or import a new module, use the **+** button on the toolbar or use the *Alt + Insert* keyboard shortcut:

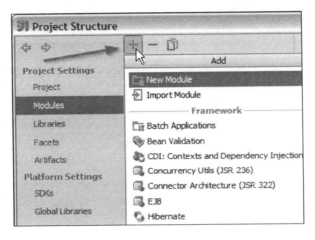

Of course, you can add a new module to an existing project. Modules can also depend on each other—they can be added as dependencies for other modules. To create such a dependency, click on **Module Dependency...** and use the *Alt + Insert* keyboard shortcut, as shown in the following screenshot:

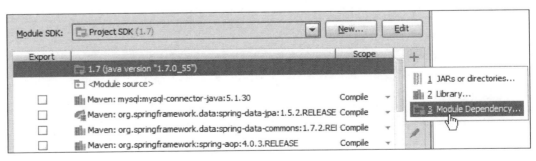

In the next dialog box, select one or more modules that the current modules should depend on, as shown in the following screenshot:

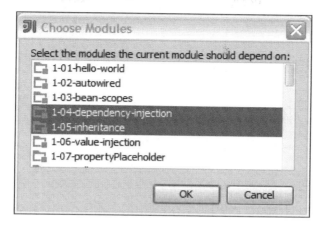

IntelliJ IDEA stores module configurations in a file with the `.iml` extension. You can put the `.iml` files into version control to be able to share module specific configuration easily.

It might be worth mentioning that if you are using external build tool such as Maven or Gradle in your project, these files will be regenerated by opening or importing the project. In this case, it's better not to store IntelliJ IDEA module configuration files in the version control system.

Folders

The structure of the module is represented by the folders on the disk. It begins with **Content Root**. You can have multiple content roots in the module. Each content root can have different types of folders:

- `Sources`: These folders contain your source files. They will be analyzed and indexed, and they are available to the compiler. If you develop in Java, the structure of the subfolders will match the package hierarchy.

- `Tests`: This is the location of your unit tests. The files from these folders will be compiled and available to run tests. The compile output will go to the same output folder as for the `Sources` folders. The source code in the `Sources` folder is visible to the code in the `Tests` folder, but not vice versa. We will discuss running unit tests in *Chapter 7, Red or Green? Test Your Code*.

- **Excluded**: The contents of the `Excluded` folders will not be indexed by IntelliJ IDEA. It means that you will not get parameter completion hints for source files contained in the folder of that type. IDE will know nothing about files in such folder and will ignore it. The compiler output directory, `target`, is excluded by default. The excluded directories and their contents are also not displayed in the tree structure in the **Project** tool window. It is usually good to exclude folder with large files which you don't want to be indexed, for example, logfiles.

> Indexing large files can slow down your IDE, so think about excluding them.

- **Resources**: Files in the resource folders will be simply copied untouched to the output directory during the compiling process. Store your configuration, properties, and static resources here. For a project imported from Maven, the Maven compiler will do resource filtering based on the configuration in `pom.xml` and the contents of these folders will be changed.

- **Test Resources**: This is similar to the `Resources` folders, but it's used for unit tests.

To set up the content root and folder types, open the **Project Structure** dialog box, select the desired module, and switch to the first tab, **Sources**. In the following screenshot, you can see that we add or pick the content root and then mark a folder with the appropriate folder type:

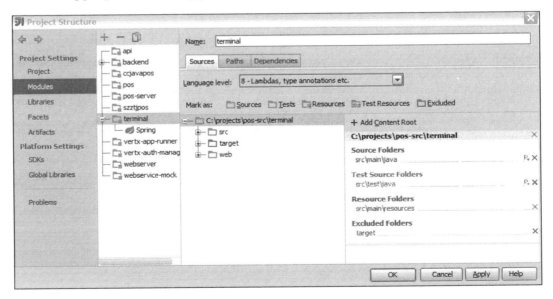

You can also mark a folder with the specified type by using the context menu, which can be accessed using the right-mouse button or using the respective keyboard shortcut, as shown here:

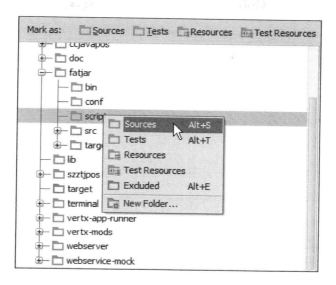

Libraries

A library is set of compiled code or resources that the module uses during compilation or runtime. If you develop in Java, this will be the set of class files enclosed in the JAR and ZIP files or directories. On the other hand, if you develop in other languages such as JavaScript, for instance, the library will consist of one or more JavaScript files similar to Angular.js or React.js.

The libraries are defined on the following three levels:

- **Global (IDE) level**: The global libraries will be shared by all projects. Use this level to set up the common libraries that you use across all of your projects, such as Apache Commons or Google Guava.

- **Project level**: The project libraries are common for all of the modules in the project. Use this to set up the library that will be used by more than one module.

- **Module level**: The library that will be recognized only by the module in which it is defined. Use this level to set up the library, which is only appropriate to a specific module.

When you set up the library, include the library source and documentation. IntelliJ IDEA will use this to provide you with hints such as parameters completion and API documentation during the coding process.

As with modules, you can add or remove the library from the project at any time using the **Project Structure** dialog box, by navigating to **File | Project structure**.

To add the project level library, click on **Libraries** and then click on the green plus icon. Alternatively, use the keyboard shortcut *Alt + Insert* as shown here:

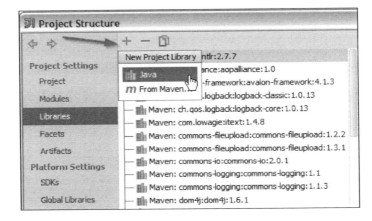

Creating the library using the **From Maven...** option is a brilliant feature that makes the creation of simple projects much easier. Just enter the name of the library you are looking for in the dialog box and use the keyboard shortcut *Shift + Enter*, as shown in the following screenshot:

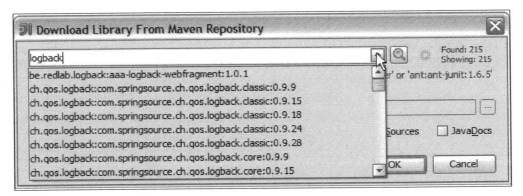

You don't need to search for and download the library manually from the Internet any more. Pick the required library from the drop-down list and IntelliJ IDEA will do it for you automatically.

To add a library on the module level, select the module, switch to the **Dependencies** tab, and then click the green plus icon or use the keyboard shortcut *Alt* + *Insert* as shown here:

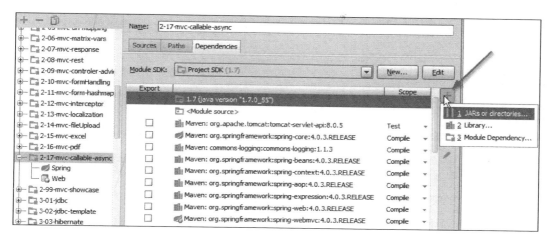

Actually, when it comes to Java development, managing libraries manually can be a painful process. I highly recommend using a dependency manager such as Maven, Gradle, or Ivy to set up the libraries. Maven build files are first-class citizens in IntelliJ IDEA. If you import the Maven project, the IDE will parse the build file and manage the libraries list automatically. We will talk about importing Maven projects later in this chapter.

Facets

Think about facets as an extension or as the "nature" of the module. Facets add support for frameworks and technologies to your module. When you add the facet to the module, IntelliJ IDEA will recognize the particular technology, language, or framework and then give you proper support. This support will consist of hints and helpers in the editor, availability of new tool windows, or the possibility of downloading framework libraries. For instance, the Spring facet allows you to navigate between Spring XML configuration files with *Ctrl* + mouse click, displays the autowiring icons, and lets you navigate to the autowired dependencies in your Java code. If you don't enable the Spring facet, you don't get any of that awesome functionality.

Some of the facets available in the IDE are Android, Web, Struts, Spring, Hibernate, and so on.

Facets can be added to the module manually using the **Project Structure** dialog box, or they can be detected by IntelliJ IDEA. To add the facet manually, switch to the **Facets** section and click on the green plus icon or use the keyboard shortcut *Alt + Insert* as shown here:

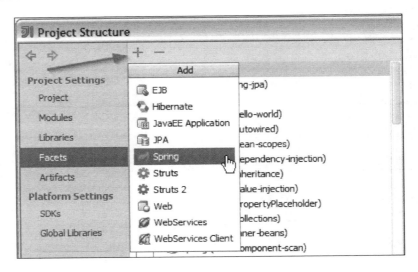

IntelliJ IDEA scans the module source code, and if it finds the file characteristic of a certain framework, it suggest the matching facet. Just click on the **Configure** link to create facets.

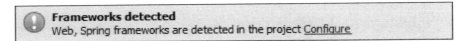

IntelliJ IDEA will then display the facet configuration dialog box, for example, the **Setup Frameworks** dialog box where you can set up the new facet, as shown in the following screenshot:

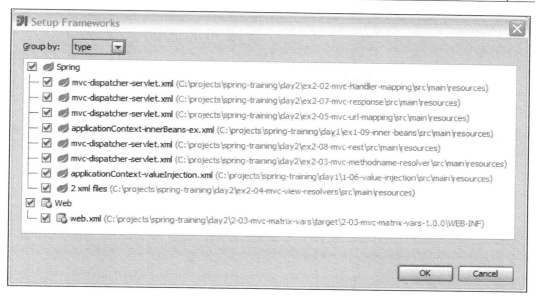

Note that a single module can have multiple facets. Expand the module branch to see the facets contained in the module, as shown in the following screenshot:

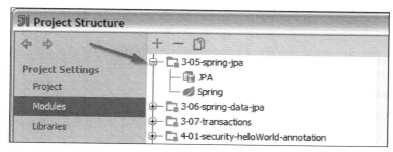

The module with two facets

Artifacts

Artifacts refer to the output of the project. Think about the artifact as a recipe that can be used to create and package the output. This can be a simple JAR resulting from compiling the Java module or a very complex, deployable file such as Java EE **Enterprise ARchive (EAR)**.

If you're using Maven, Gradle, or a similar build tool, you don't need to bother about manually creating artifacts—IntelliJ IDEA will create the desired artifacts automatically. There is also another advantage of using the external build tool: you will be able to build and package your project outside of the IDE. This can be useful when deploying the application or running the build in the continuous integration system. We will focus on the external build process in *Chapter 6, Building Your Project*. Anyhow, when required, you can create artifacts manually in the IDE. To add and remove artifacts, use the **Project Structure** dialog. You can either choose the predefined artifact type, for example, **Web Application: Archive** to create the `.war` file, or select **Other** to create custom one, as shown in the following screenshot:

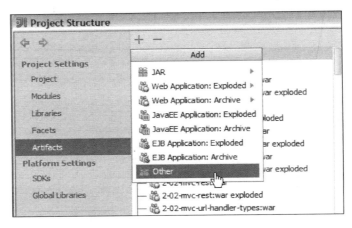

To set up the contents of artifact, pick the item (let it be library, module, or another artifact from the **Available Elements** list) and drag your artifact contents to the left.

Any item has the context menu available when you right-click on it, we can present the default predefined locations in the artifact for that item. This is shown in the following screenshot:

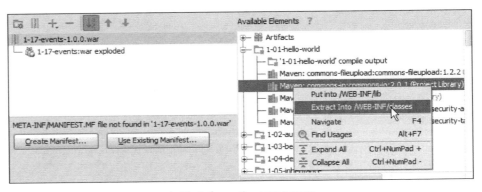

Artifact element's context menu

You can double-click on the element to put it in the default predefined place within the artifact.

To see precisely what will be included in the output, select the **Show content of elements** checkbox. You will see which files and directories will actually go to the generated output as shown here:

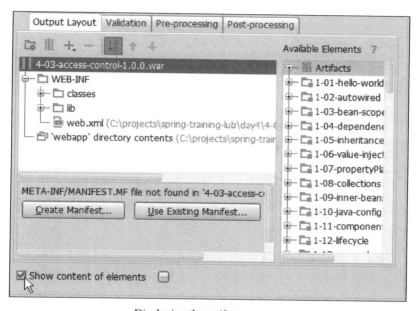

Displaying the artifact contents

Once defined, artifacts are available in the **Build artifacts** command in the **Build** menu. We will more about building the module in *Chapter 6, Building Your Project*.

 There is actually no limit for the number of artifacts in the project; create as many as you like!

Creating a project

Now that we have the most important IntelliJ IDEA project concepts explained, we can create or import the project. Let's start with the creating a completely new project.

Creating a new project from scratch

To create the new project, select **New Project** form the **File** menu or use the standard *Alt* shortcuts for operation on menus: *Alt + F*, *Alt + N*, and then press *Enter*. You will be presented with the **New Project** wizard window, as shown in the following screenshot:

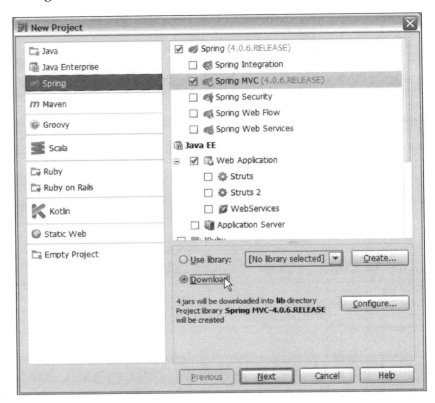

In the **New Project** wizard window, choose the technology you would like to develop with. Depending on the selected option, the dialog will change to allow you to enter settings that are more specific. For Java projects, for example, you will be able to select the framework you would like to be included in the project. Any framework needs a library of classes—IntelliJ IDEA can reuse the existing library or automatically download the proper library from the Internet. The newest version of the library is selected by default, but you can change this using the **Configure** button.

If you cannot see your preferred language or framework in the **New Project** dialog box, refer to the *Pick your plugins* section in the previous chapter to find the plugin for the language and framework of your choice.

When you select Maven as a starting point for your project, you can also pick the Maven archetype IntelliJ IDEA will use as the project base. This is shown in the following screenshot:

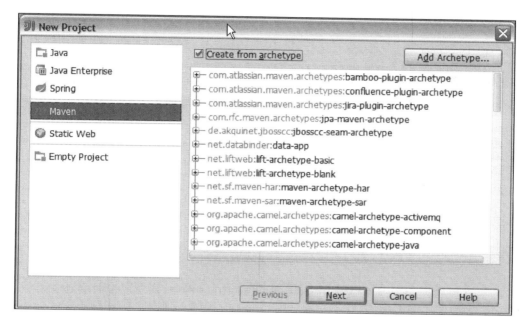

The next few windows of the **New Project** wizard will vary according to the option selected at the beginning. It will be the selection of SDK for Java, Scala, Ruby, and Python projects or other framework-specific options.

The last page of the wizard allows you to set paths for the project and, optionally, the project format, module location, and module name.

If the project you are creating is the first one, you will probably need to set up the SDK for the project. Click on the **New** button in the **Project SDK** section and point to the home directory of your JDK, as shown in the following screenshot:

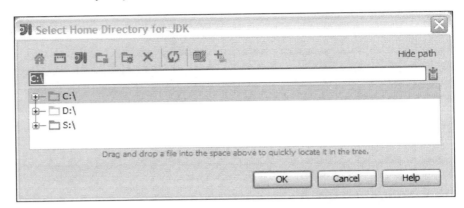

The first three buttons in the file chooser section of the toolbar are **Home Directory**, **Desktop Directory**, and **Project Directory**.

You can use them as quick shortcuts to get straight to the desired directory. They are very handy and appear in every file selection dialog of IntelliJ IDEA.

When you click on **Finish**, in almost all of the cases, IntelliJ IDEA will create a project containing a module. We talked about modules earlier in the *Modules* section of this chapter.

Importing the existing project

The existing project can be imported into the IDE in two ways: from the existing sources or from the build model (it can be Maven or Gradle, for example). You can also import the Eclipse project into IntelliJ IDEA. For NetBeans, currently there is no such functionality in the IDE. However, if you would like to import the NetBeans project, you can create a new project with the existing sources.

To start the import process, click on **Import project** from the **File** menu. In the next dialog, choose the existing directory or the build file (`pom.xml` or `build.gradle`), as shown in the following screenshot:

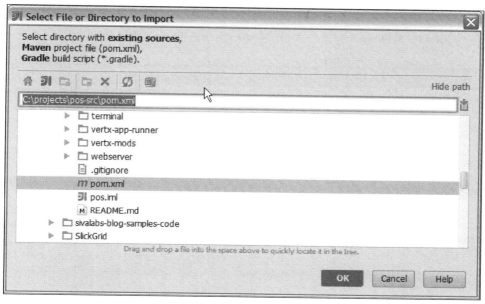

Selecting the directory or the model to import

For Maven projects, you can also use the **Open** option from the **File** menu and then point to the `pom.xml` file of your project. The IDE will then import the project automatically without any additional import dialogs to fill out. Basically, IntelliJ IDEA treats Maven-based projects as first-class citizens, equal to its own project format.

If you decide to import a project from the existing Maven model, IntelliJ IDEA will create the project configuration matching the pom structure; project modules will be shaped from the pom modules and dependencies defined in the pom file will be set up as project or module libraries. The Maven output directory, `target`, will be excluded automatically by default. If you leave **Use Maven output directories** checked, IntelliJ IDEA will reuse Maven output directories as the compiler output—`target` or `classes` by default.

When you create project from the existing sources, IntelliJ IDEA will not copy the files anywhere. It will just create project in the directory of your choice; the existing sources will stay where they are.

It's good to have the **Automatically download Sources and Documentation** option checked; IntelliJ IDEA will try to download the library sources and API documentation to assist you better in the editor. The option can be seen in the following screenshot:

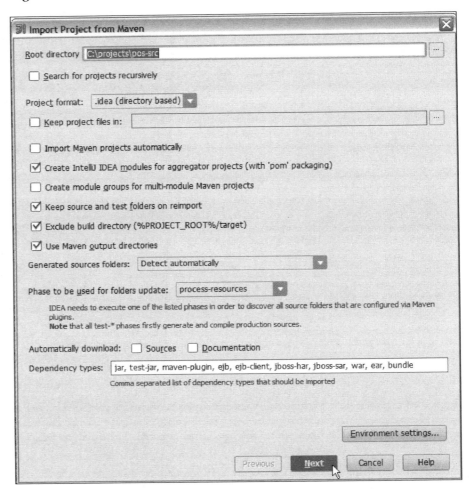

When you select **Import Maven projects automatically**, changes in the pom.xml file get automatically synchronized with the IntelliJ IDEA's project structure each time your pom.xml file is changed. It should be noted that when working with large projects, this synchronization can take a while. I suggest that you should disable this option when you are working on such projects.

If you choose to import the project from the existing sources, select the directory containing your project and then select the **Create project from existing sources** option, as shown in the following screenshot:

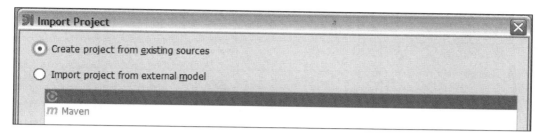

First, IntelliJ IDEA will scan the directory recursively for source files and libraries. The next scan will look for files specific to any known frameworks; IntelliJ IDEA will try to generate the facets if any of such file is found. Review these findings carefully; IntelliJ IDEA will try to form the project structure from them.

Then, open **Project Structure** from the **File** menu and review the generated project structure again. Look for the proper modules, libraries, and facets definitions. You can always tweak the project structure here. Feel free to modify it: add or remove modules, mark the folders with proper type, or set up the facets.

Project format

IntelliJ IDEA can store project configuration files in two alternative formats. The first one is directory-based—it is newer, recommended, and the default. The second format is file-based. You can choose the desired format in the project setup or project import wizard.

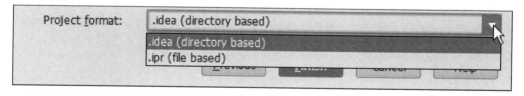

The directory-based format

When you choose a directory-based format, IntelliJ IDEA will create the .idea directory in your project folder. This directory will contain all project-wide configuration settings in a number of XML files. Specific settings are grouped in different files: compiler.xml will contain the compiler settings, modules.xml will contain the module setup, and so on.

You can throw files from the .idea folder or even the whole .idea folder into the version control system if you like with the exception of workspace.xml and tasks.xml. These files hold your personal settings, such as the tasks list, the list of opened files, local history, version control setup, and the running configurations. If you are using Maven, it's better to just throw the pom.xml file into the version control system and let IntelliJ IDEA do the rest.

The file-based format

If you decide to set up the project using a file-based format, IntelliJ IDEA will create two project files for you with the extensions .ipr and .iws. The first one, .ipr file, will contain project-specific settings. On the other hand, the .iws file will contain your personal settings, similar to the workspace.xml in the directory-based setup. IntelliJ IDEA will automatically put the .iws file on the ignore list of your version control system.

You should not put the .iws file into the version control system.

Later on, if you decide that you want to switch to the directory-based format, use the **Save as Directory-Based Format** option from the **File** menu. IntelliJ IDEA will convert your project files and reopen the project. After the project reopens, you are safe to delete the .ipr and .iws files.

The directory-based format versus the file-based format

The rationale behind the new directory-based format was to reduce merge conflicts that occurred a lot more with the file-based format. Since the settings are spread over a dozen files instead of being located in a single file, the chances of merge conflicts are somewhat reduced. The features of the directory-based format are as follows:

- You can decide what group of settings you want to share with your team using the version control system; just put the file you do not want to share in the ignore list.

- It is easier to find specific settings; the files are small and have meaningful filenames.

- IntelliJ IDEA will recognize the directory containing the `.idea` subdirectory as a project in the **File** dialog box. You do not need to select the `.ipr` file manually.

I believe there is no reason to use file-based configuration anymore. So let's stick to the directory-based configuration.

Summary

Project definition in IntelliJ IDEA can seem complex at first sight, but you will find that it is very flexible and well designed. In this chapter, you learned about the project concepts, such as modules, libraries, facets, and artifacts. We looked at project creation and the process of importing. From now on, you will be able to create, import, and tweak your project structure in the IDE easily.

In the next chapter, we will talk about the core of IntelliJ IDEA, that is, the editor, and start actual coding.

3
The Editor

The editor is the core and strongest feature of IntelliJ IDEA. This is the part of the IDE where IntelliJ IDEA really shines and shows its huge potential. In this chapter, we will have an overview of the editor, set it up, use state of the art code completion and hints, discuss how to effectively navigate through the files, quickly display code documentation, and get to know how to compare files and folders. We will also set up and use powerful features of Live Templates. You will spend most of your development time in the editor, so we will focus on productivity tips and the most useful keyboard shortcuts throughout the chapter.

We will cover the following topics in this chapter:

- An overview of the editor and setup
- Navigating in the editor
- The editor basics
- Using Live Templates and postfix completion
- Comparing files and folders
- Looking for help

An overview of the editor and setup

The IntelliJ IDEA editor supports all of the standard features, such as file tabs, bookmarks, and syntax highlighting. The main parts of the editor workspace are the editor itself, tabs, gutter area, status bar, and scroll bar.

The gutter area

The gutter area is placed vertically on the left-hand side of the editor. It presents additional information about the code you are working on. The gutter is very powerful and an interactive tool. You can click on an element in the gutter to execute the action at any time. You can also hover your mouse over a symbol to see additional information or a hint.

In the gutter area, you will find various icons that identify the code structure. When you are editing the Java class or interface, for example, the gutter will show the **overrides** or **is overridden by** icons. Clicking on these icons will list the related, appropriate files, allowing you to open them in the editor instantly. If you work with the specific framework and have plugins installed, there will be more icons available in the gutter. For example, if you are working on the Spring project, the icons in the gutter will allow you to jump from the class implementing Spring components to places where they are used by Spring and vice versa, as shown in the following screenshot:

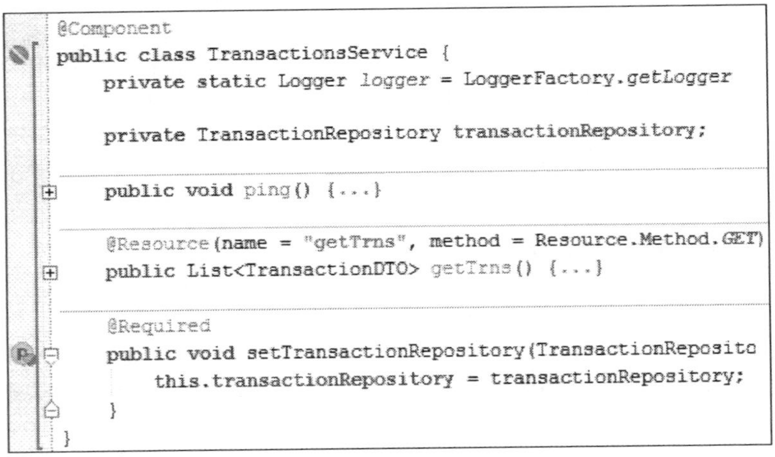

```
@Component
public class TransactionsService {
    private static Logger logger = LoggerFactory.getLogger

    private TransactionRepository transactionRepository;

    public void ping() {...}

    @Resource(name = "getTrns", method = Resource.Method.GET)
    public List<TransactionDTO> getTrns() {...}

    @Required
    public void setTransactionRepository(TransactionReposito
        this.transactionRepository = transactionRepository;
    }
}
```

The gutter with the symbols and code-folding icons

If the file being edited is under the version control system and becomes modified, the gutter will show the *change marker* in the modified lines as shown in the following screenshot. Clicking on the change marker allows you to rollback the change or show the difference. You will learn more about working with version control in *Chapter 9, Working with Your Team*.

```
  $scope.loadGrid = function () {
          le.log('loadGid');
  Rollback

  ⬆  ⬇  ◀  ⌂  ▯

      $scope.loader = gridService.loader("/api/transactions/getTrns", 50);

      $scope.grid = new Slick.Grid("#transactionList", $scope.loader.data,

      $scope.grid.onViewportChanged.subscribe(function (e, args) {
          var vp = $scope.grid.getViewport();
          $scope.loader.ensureData(vp.top, vp.bottom);
      });
```

The version control tab on the gutter

The gutter also contains the code folding icons. The code-folding feature can be used to collapse the source code blocks and reduce them visually to a single line. The icon with the *minus* sign indicates the beginning of the code block that can be folded. When folded, the code block is represented by the ellipsis mark in the editor and the icons with the *plus* mark on the gutter. You can hover the mouse over the ellipsis mark in the editor to see the content of the folded block.

At any time, clicking on the icon or ellipsis mark will expand the source code block. You can also use the following keyboard shortcuts:

Action	PC shortcut	Mac shortcut
Expand/collapse the code block	*Ctrl + + / - key on the numpad*	*cmd + Shift + .*
Expand all	*Ctrl + Shift + + key on the numpad*	*cmd + Shift + =*
Collapse all	*Ctrl + Shift + - key on the numpad*	*cmd + Shift + -*

Additionally, the code-folding options can be accessed by navigating to **Code |
Folding** or from the context menu in the editor, as shown in the following screenshot:

```java
public ReflectingServiceHandler(String serviceName, Logger logger, ObjectMapper om, Object serviceObject) {
    this.logger = logger;
    this.om = om;
    this.serviceObject = serviceObject;
    this.serviceName = serviceName;
    serviceMethods = new HashMap<>();

    for (Method method : serviceObject.getClass().getDeclaredMethods()) {
        if (method.isAnnotationPresent(Resource.class)) {
            Resource resource = method.getAnnotation(Resource.class);
            addOrCreateRef(resource.method(), resource.name(), method);
        }
    }
}

private void addOrCreateRef(Resource.Method webMethod, String name, Method serviceMethod) {
    if (serviceMethods.containsKey(webMethod)) {
        serviceMethods.get(webMethod).put(name, serviceMethod);
    } else {
        HashMap<String, Method> serviceMethodNameValueMap = new HashMap<>();
        serviceMethodNameValueMap.put(name, serviceMethod);
        serviceMethods.put(webMethod, serviceMethodNameValueMap);
    }
}
```

The code-folding icons

When you hover the mouse over the ellipsis of the collapsed block, IntelliJ
IDEA will display its preview in a pop-up window. If the code-fold
marker towards the upper side is outside the visible area of the editor,
hover the mouse over the lower marker. IntelliJ IDEA will display the
whole block in the pop-up window, as shown in the following screenshot:

```
controllers.controller('transactionsController', function ($scope, $location, $log,
    $scope.notification = humane.create({baseCls: 'humane-bigbox', timeout: 1000});
    $scope.notification.error = $scope.notification.spawn({addnCls: 'humane-bigbox-
    $scope.gridOptions = gridService.getDefaultGridOptions();

    $scope.loadGrid = function () {
        console.log('loadGid');
        $scope.loader = gridService.loader("/api/transactions/getTrns", 50);

        $scope.grid = new Slick.Grid("#transactionList", $scope.loader.data, $scope
```

The preview for the code outside the editor area

IntelliJ IDEA can fold some predefined code blocks, such as file headers, import
sections, and anonymous classes, automatically. You can also switch the code folding
outline completely off if you don't plan to use it. To set up the code folding behavior,
go to **IDE Settings | Editor | Code folding** in the **Settings** dialog box. Select the
desired code block types to have them collapsed by default; for example, you can
have anonymous classes collapsed by default.

The code-folding feature is extremely useful if you analyze the legacy source code and would like to hide specific blocks to get a better understanding of the code structure.

If you have a debugging configuration set up, you use the gutter to set the breakpoints in the code. Just click on the gutter at the line you would like the debugger to stop. The big red dot will indicate the breakpoint setup. You will learn more about debugging your project in *Chapter 8, Squash'em – The Debugger*.

```java
@Resource(name = "getDevices", method = Resource.Method.GET)
@SuppressWarnings("unused")
public List<Device> getDevices() {
    logger.info("loading devices");
    return devicesRepository.findAll(new Sort(Sort.Direction.DESC,
}
```

The breakpoint indicators

The Status bar

Information about the file currently being edited is shown at the bottom of the editor, in the status bar. The information provided here is the current line number and column number, the line separator type (CR (Mac) or CRLF (Windows), for example), and the character encoding being used. The line separator and file encoding can be modified. Just click on the encoding to see the list of available encodings and select the desired encoding to use. If the encoding switch requires the file to be modified, IntelliJ IDEA will ask to reload or convert the file, as shown in the following screenshot:

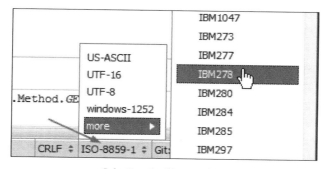

Selecting the file encoding

The little lock icon represents the file's read-only status. If it's unlocked, you can modify the file; if it's locked, the file is in read-only mode:

The file writing mode indicator

The status bar also indicates that IntelliJ IDEA is currently performing some lengthy process such as building indices:

While building indices, some of IntelliJ IDEA's features are disabled for a while, such as navigating to **Go To Class** or **Find Usages**.

When you code, IntelliJ IDEA runs the code analysis continuously to support you with visual hints and catch potential bugs in the code. This feature is called code inspection. We will discuss this aspect in the *Code inspection* section in this chapter. On the status bar, there is an icon of a little guy wearing the Billycock. Clicking on this icon allows you to change the current code inspections profile to be more or less restrictive, as shown in the following screenshot:

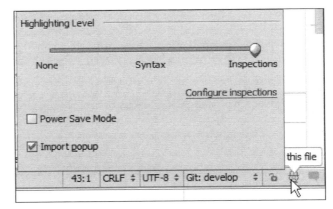

Setting the code inspections profile

If you use GIT for version control, the status bar will present the current branch of the project. Clicking on the branch label will open a list of local and remote branches and allow you to quickly switch to another branch or create a new one, as shown in the following screenshot. We will cover more of this subject in *Chapter 9, Working with Your Team*.

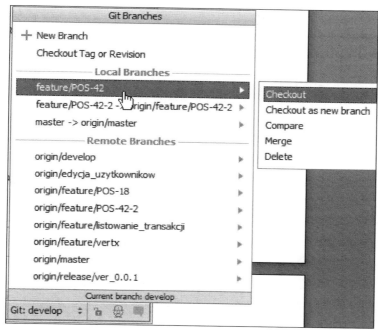

The GIT branches menu

Tabs

The IntelliJ IDEA editor is tab-based. Every file you open in the editor will have its own tab. The tabs can be rearranged by dragging them with your mouse.

The tab bar can have either top, bottom, left, or right placement in the workspace. The setting for the tabs placement can be accessed by navigating to **Settings | Editor | General | Editor Tabs** in the **Settings** dialog box.

To start working on the file, select its tab to bring it to the front. Every tab has a context menu that is available when you right-click on it. Using this menu allows you to execute file-specific actions, such as closing the file, closing the other files, adding the file to the Favorites list, renaming files, displaying the local history of the file, displaying version control commands, and so on:

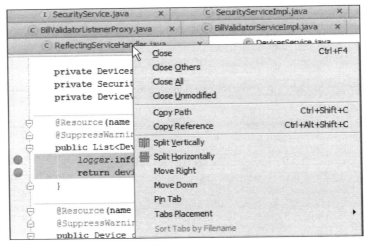

The tab context menu

There is a nice feature available in the tab context menu: editor splitting. You can select **Split Horizontally** or **Split Vertically** to be able to work on two or more files in the editor at the same time. You can also work on different parts of the same file. You may find it useful to set up keyboard shortcuts for this. Good candidates here can be *Ctrl + Alt + Shift + H* and *Ctrl + Alt + Shift + V* (PC) and *control + Shift + H* and *control + Shift + V* (Mac); they're memorable and not already taken. It's much faster to use keyboard shortcut rather than the mouse.

 The editor can be divided almost infinitely, so your display size and resolution are the only boundary.

As we discussed earlier, tabs are optional in IntelliJ IDEA. If you memorize the keyboard shortcuts to navigate through the opened files, you can switch them off in the **Settings** dialog box if you like. We will cover the details of navigation in the *Navigating in the editor* section.

Scratches

Apart from working on ordinary disk-based files, you can work with scratches in IntelliJ IDEA. It is a very handy feature that helps you experiment and create prototypes without modifying your project or creating new files. Depending on the type of scratch, IntelliJ IDEA will provide all of its coding assistance, such as code completion and hints, in a way that is similar to the regular file. To create a scratch, choose **New Scratch File** from the **Tools** menu or use *control + Alt + Shift + Insert* (PC) or *Ctrl + Shift + N* (Mac) and then select the type of scratch:

 Scratches are not saved or preserved when you close or switch to another project.

Scrollbar

IntelliJ IDEA analyses your source files all the time. If it detects some potential problems, it marks the corresponding lines with warning (yellow) or error (red) marks on the right scrollbar. These are called stripe marks. Stripe marks are also used to mark the search results, modified lines if using version control, TODO marks, and so on. You can navigate to the next error in the editor by pressing *F2*, or *Shift + F2* if you want to go to the previous error, as shown in the following screenshot. We will discuss this more fully later in this chapter.

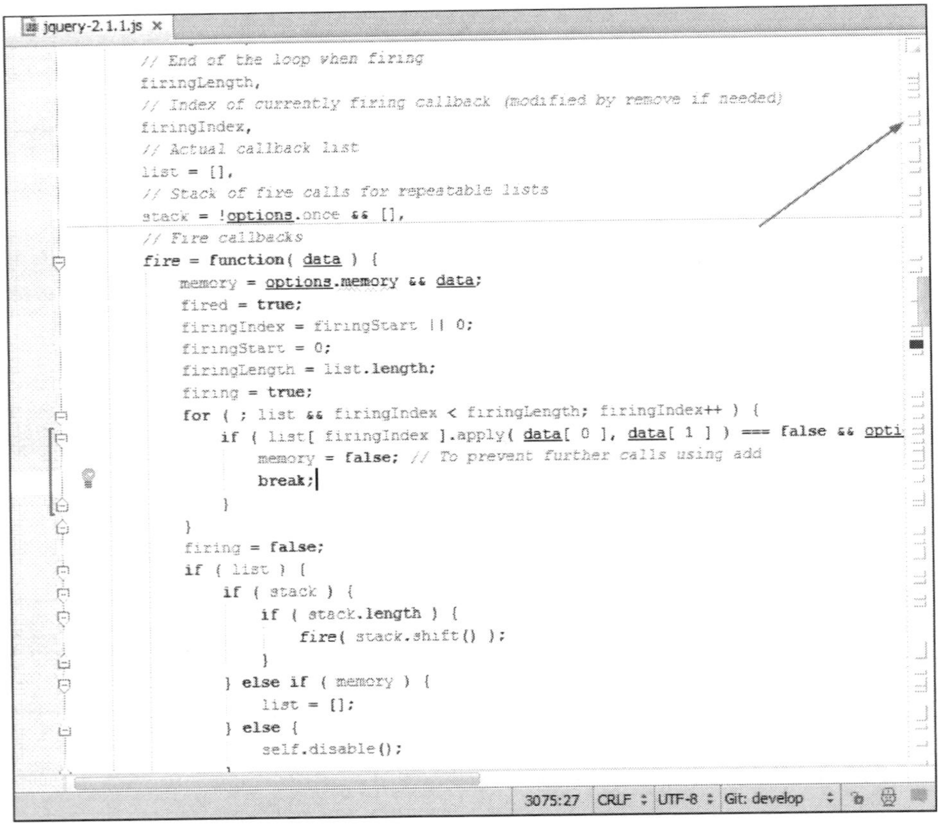

The stripe marks on the scrollbar

Clicking on each of these marks will make an instant jump to the marked line. You can also hover the mouse over the marks to see the description of the stripe marks, as shown in the following screenshot:

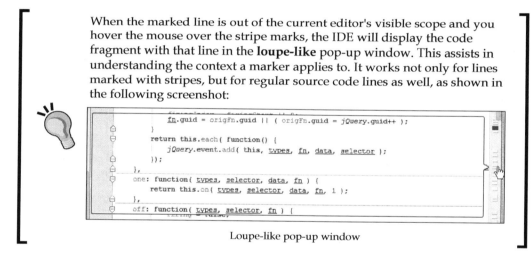

The problem descriptions for the stripe marks

You can configure colors or add other types of stripe marks by navigating to **IDE Settings | Editor | Colors and Fonts | General** in the **Settings** window.

> When the marked line is out of the current editor's visible scope and you hover the mouse over the stripe marks, the IDE will display the code fragment with that line in the **loupe-like** pop-up window. This assists in understanding the context a marker applies to. It works not only for lines marked with stripes, but for regular source code lines as well, as shown in the following screenshot:

Loupe-like pop-up window

Now, as we have gone through the editor's features, let's move on to navigating between files, between types, and within a single file.

Navigating in the editor

When working on a project, you work on a set of files. You switch between them a lot, so knowledge of how to navigate efficiently between files, types, or methods is essential to speed up development. Basically, the faster you switch between files, the more productive you are.

Navigating between files

IntelliJ IDEA provides a switcher between opened files and tool windows. It's similar to the application switcher in your operating system such as *Alt + Tab* on Windows or *cmd + Tab* on the Mac. The switcher in IntelliJ IDEA is available by using the *Ctrl + Tab* keyboard shortcut. If the switcher pop-up is visible, keep the *Ctrl* key pressed and use the *Tab* key (or the cursor + up and down arrow keys) to select the desired tool window or file. In the switcher, you will see only the files that are currently opened in the editor, as shown in the following screenshot:

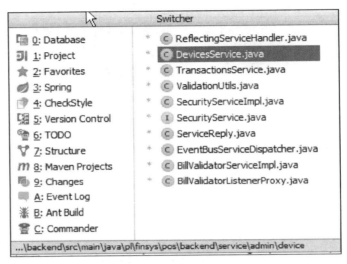

The tab switcher

You can also use *Alt* + the left arrow key to switch to the previous tab and *Alt* + the right arrow key to move to the next tab. The tab switcher can be helpful when you start working with the project. However, later, when your working set of files stabilizes and is more or less defined, there are many more powerful switching methods to select the file in the editor; these include as **Recent files** and **Recently edited files**.

The **Recent files** dialog box is a real time-saver. Available via *Ctrl + E* in Windows (*cmd + E* in Mac), it opens by default the last accessed file. You can also select any tool window in this dialog box, just as you could in the *Tab* switcher, as shown in the following screenshot:

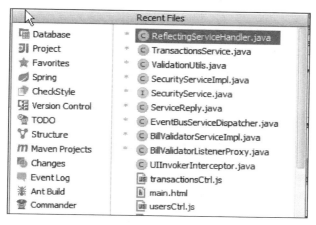

The Recent Files dialog box

An even more powerful file switcher is the **Recently edited files** dialog box, available via *Shift + Ctrl + E* (PC) or *Shift + cmd + E* (Mac). It is visually identical to the **Recent Files** dialog box, but presents only the files you are most interested in, that is, files that were recently modified. This dialog box will highlight the files currently open. Please note that it will not include the file you are currently in.

If you become familiar with the **Recent files** and **Recently edited files** dialog boxes, you will find the normal *Tab* switcher pretty useless.

It's good to increase the number of recent files in these dialog boxes. To do this, navigate to **IDE Settings | Editor | Recent files limit** in the **Settings** window. As we already know from the first chapter, any list-based dialog box can be filtered simply by typing the characters you want to find—this applies to the recent files dialog box as well.

If you install IntelliJ IDEA for the first time, you will see **Navigation Bar** at the top of the editor, as shown in the following screenshot. It's visible by default, but most of the time it's not very useful and takes precious screen space.

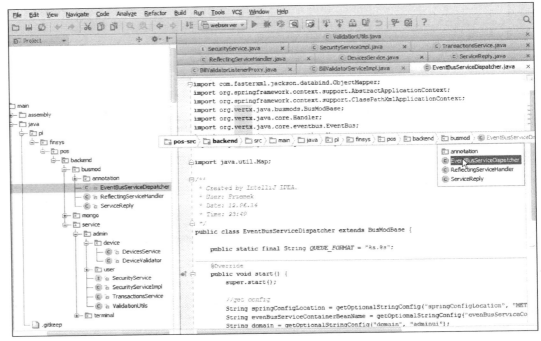

The floating navigation bar

You can switch Navigation Bar on or off by navigating to **View | Navigation Bar**. It becomes useful when shown on demand, using the *Alt + Home* shortcut. It will display as a floating bar over the editor and allow opening files from the directory structure of the project. As with almost every IntelliJ IDEA component, **Navigation Bar** has the context menu available by right-clicking. The context menu contains folder- or file-specific actions, such as **Compile** or **Reformat code**.

You learned a couple of file switching methods, but there are some more. One of them is a very useful file switching action: **Navigate file**. Execute it by using *Ctrl + Shift + N* (PC) or *cmd + Shift + O* (Mac). A small dialog box will pop up waiting for you to start typing the filename. You can use wildcards such as * to represent any number of characters and ? to represent exactly one character.

In addition to wildcards, you can type the first few letters of each word in PascalCase, camelCase, kebab-case, or snake_case. For example, to navigate to the `src/some/package/BillAcceptorService.java` path just use `BAS` or `bas`. If you have two files of the same name in different packages/folders, you can include the folder portion of the path as well; `s/p/bas` will show `src/some/package/BillAcceptorService.java` but not `src/other/package/BillAcceptorService.java`. The search is not case-sensitive, but the case will be considered if there's more than one file that matches the pattern you type. For example, if file A matches the capitalization of your search and file B does not, file A will be listed first. It's a super powerful feature.

The list of matching files will be shown. Just select the file to open it in the editor. If you would like to include non-project files (from the external libraries or resources) in the search, mark the corresponding checkbox or just use the keyboard shortcut again. If you decide to include only specific file types in the search, click on the little funnel icon and select the desired file types, as shown in the following screenshot:

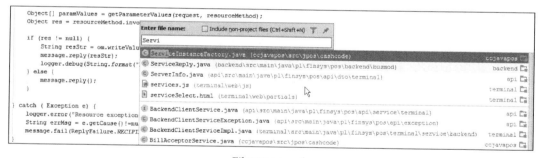

Filename search

IntelliJ IDEA is not just a text file editor, but also a full-fledged development environment. The IDE knows about the types of development environment defined in your project and allows you to navigate between them. To navigate to a class, use *Ctrl + N* (PC) or *cmd + O* (Mac) to display the **Navigate Class** dialog box. The pop-up will be almost the same as **Navigate file**, but will show classes instead of files. Similarly, using the shortcut again will include non-project classes and the funnel icon narrows the search results according to the chosen type, as shown in the following screenshot:

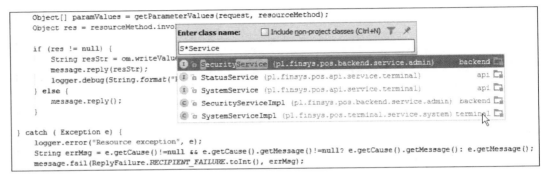

Class search

If you would like to open a file with a particular symbol (such as a method or field name, for example), execute the **Navigate symbol** action, by using the following shortcut: *Ctrl + Alt + Shift + N* (PC) or *cmd + Alt + Shift + N* (Mac). Again, the same rules apply; just start typing to find the file containing the specified symbol. You can also use the first letters from the CamelCase symbol name, exactly in the same way as navigating to a file. Hit the shortcut again to include symbols that are specific to non-projects, such as classes from external libraries, as shown in the following screenshot:

Symbol search

There are three more navigation shortcuts, specific to object-oriented languages. If you develop in Java, for example, you may find them very useful. To navigate to a file with a class declaration, use *Ctrl + B* (PC) or *cmd + B* (Mac). It's the equivalent of *Ctrl* + left-click of the mouse (PC) or *cmd* + left-click of the mouse (Mac). Alternatively, you can also use the *F4* shortcut, for jumping to the source.

To list the implementations of the type, use *Ctrl + Alt + B* (PC) or *cmd + option + B* (Mac). To quickly go to the superclass of the class you opened in the editor, use *Ctrl + U* (PC) or *cmd + U* (Mac). It might be worth mentioning that the same set of shortcuts applies to methods as well.

You probably do many unit tests for your code. To quickly switch from the file being edited to a unit test, use *Shift + Ctrl + T* (PC) or *Shift + cmd + T* (Mac).

IntelliJ IDEA supports the feature available in almost all modern IDEs—bookmarks. To place a bookmark at a specified line, press *F11* (PC) or *F3* (Mac). You can also use *Ctrl + F11* (PC) or *Alt + F3* (Mac) to place a bookmark with its mnemonic. The mnemonic will be displayed in the gutter area and can be in the form of a number or letter; it lets you distinguish between different bookmarks. To display the list of bookmarks, press *Shift + F11* (PC) or *cmd + F3* (Mac); the output is shown in the following screenshot:

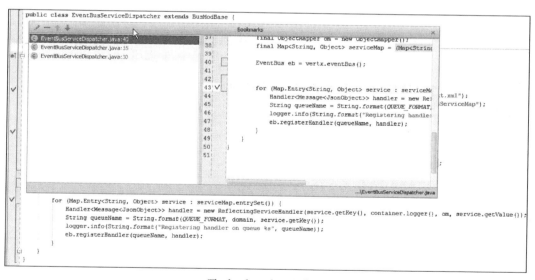

The bookmarks window

The following table summarizes file switching actions and associated shortcuts:

Action	PC shortcut	Mac shortcut
Switch tab (opened files)	*Ctrl + Tab*	*cmd + Tab*
View recent files	*Ctrl + E*	*cmd + E*
View recently modified files	*Ctrl + Shift + E*	*cmd + Shift + E*
Navigate to a file	*Ctrl + Shift + N*	*cmd + Shift + O*
Navigate to a class	*Ctrl + N*	*cmd + O*
Navigate to a symbol	*Ctrl + Alt + Shift + N*	*cmd + Alt + O*
Navigate to declaration	*Ctrl + B*	*cmd + B*
Navigate to super	*Ctrl + U*	*cmd + U*
Navigate to implementations	*Ctrl + Alt + B*	*cmd + Alt + B*
Navigate to a test	*Ctrl + Shift + T*	*cmd + Shift + T*
Place a bookmark	*F11*	*F3*
Show bookmarks	*Shift + F11*	*cmd + F3*

Now we know how to look for and open files instantly, let's look at how to navigate within a single file.

Navigating within a single file

IntelliJ IDEA supports the standard way of jumping to a specific line: *Ctrl + G* (PC) or *cmd + G* (Mac)— used as the go to line shortcut. It's useful when you know the line number you want to go to. However, if you don't, perhaps the most useful action to navigate within a single file is **File structure**. It's available in the **Navigate** menu or by using *Ctrl + F12* (PC) or *cmd + F12* (Mac). This action will display a pop-up window presenting the full file structure breakdown. This will be the method names if you are editing a Java file, or the elements tree if editing an XML file. Again, by entering a keyword using the keyboard, the list can be narrowed down to find a specific item instantly. Of course, as always, you can use wildcards and camel humps here. Using the shortcut again will turn on the additional option; for Java classes, it will include the inherited members in the list.

To quickly jump between methods in a file, use *Alt* + the up arrow key or the down arrow key (PC) or *control* + the up arrow key or the down arrow key (Mac). Take note that this shortcut is actually overridden by Mac's mission control, so you need to disable it by navigating to **System Preferences | Keyboard | Keyboard Shortcuts | Mission Control** before the user can use it in IntelliJ IDEA.

To swiftly leap between braces, use *Ctrl + {* and *Ctrl + }* (PC) or *cmd + {* and *cmd + }* (Mac). To scroll the contents of the editor without changing the current position of the cursor, use *Ctrl* + the up arrow key or the down arrow key (PC) or *cmd* + the up arrow key or the down arrow key (Mac).

We already know that, if IntelliJ IDEA detects some errors or warnings, it marks them with stripe marks. The easiest way to navigate to the next/previous error or warning is by using the *F2* and *Shift + F2* keyboard shortcuts, respectively. When you hover the cursor over the issue, you can display its details using *Ctrl + F1*. There is an editor setting that allows you to modify the behavior of *F2*, so it goes to errors first and only goes to warnings once all errors are gone. Right-click on the stripe marks area and choose **Go to high priority problems only** to have IntelliJ IDEA skip warnings, infos, and other minor issues. Choose **Go to next problem** to have the IDE jump between all detected issues:

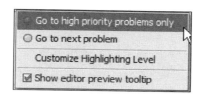

The following table summarizes navigation within a single file:

Action	PC shortcut	Mac shortcut
Go to a line	*Ctrl + G*	*cmd + L*
Check the file structure	*Ctrl + F12*	*cmd + F12*
Navigate between methods	*Alt* + up arrow key or the down arrow key	*control* + up arrow key or the down arrow key
Scroll the editor content	*Ctrl* + up arrow key or the down arrow key	*cmd* + up arrow key or the down arrow key
Navigate between braces	*Ctrl + { / }*	*cmd + { / }*
Navigate to the next error/warning	*F2*	*F2*
Navigate to the previous error/warning	*Shift + F2*	*Shift + F2*

There are two more navigation actions available in IntelliJ IDEA. I believe these are the most powerful of them all; they work within a single file and across files, as well. These actions are **Navigate back/forward** and **Navigate/Last edit location**.

The **Navigate back / forward** action is accessible by using *Ctrl + Alt* + the left arrow key (PC) or *cmd + Alt* + the left arrow key (Mac), and *Ctrl + Alt* + the right arrow key (PC) or *cmd + Alt* + the right arrow key (Mac) works just like the back and forward buttons on your Internet browser.

When you code, you very often switch to another file apart from the one currently being edited. **Navigate / Last edit location**, available by using *Ctrl + Shift + Backspace* (PC) or *cmd + Shift + Backspace* (Mac), allows you to check the other file to look something up and then instantly gets you back to your last edited line. Try it, it's a real time-saver.

> **Navigate/Last edit location** will always get you back to your latest changes in the code.

The Search Everywhere feature

The **Search Everywhere** feature, available by pressing the left *Shift* key twice, is the most potent navigation feature; it allows you to search for everything. Literally everything! Just press the shortcut to see the list of recent files. Start typing and IntelliJ IDEA will show you a list of files and symbols. Press *Shift* twice, again, to include non-project files in the search. Most importantly, the search results list will also include all the matching IDE actions and preference settings. For example, if you don't recall the shortcut for the GIT push action, just type push in the dialog box and choose the action found. It's that easy. The following screenshot shows how the window will look:

Search Everywhere in action.

The **Search Everywhere** feature is the king of all shortcuts in IntelliJ IDEA. When in doubt, just double-press the left *Shift* key and start typing!

By now, you have learned how to effectively find any place in a project where we want to make a change. We can navigate to the desired file and move freely within it. It's time to start editing the source.

The editor basics

IntelliJ IDEA's editor supports all the standard features of a text editor such as selecting text, searching, cutting, copying, and pasting. Let's start with some basic editor commands and then focus on more advanced features of IntelliJ IDEA, such as syntax-aware selection, clipboard history, code reformatting, smart code completion, and code inspections.

To duplicate a line of code (or a selected block) use *Ctrl + D* (PC) or *cmd + D* (Mac). To remove a line of code or selected block, use *Ctrl + Y* (PC) or *cmd + Y* (Mac).

Sometimes it may be useful to comment portions of code. To use the line comment, press *Ctrl + /* (PC) or *cmd + /* (Mac). If you favor the block comment, use *Shift + Ctrl + /* (PC) or *Shift + cmd + /* (Mac). IntelliJ IDEA will be aware of the programming language of the file you are editing and use the comments that are appropriate to this language. Like almost every programmer's editor, IntelliJ IDEA provides you with the option to search for text and text replace functionality.

Searching for and replacing text

To execute a text search, use the *Ctrl + F* (PC) or *cmd + F* (Mac) keyboard shortcut. The search bar will pop up at the top of the editor. Start typing the text you want to find and IntelliJ IDEA will automatically highlight all the occurrences of the text in the content of the editor, as shown in the following screenshot:

```
public String createTrn(Transaction transaction, Device terminal) {
    logger.debug("Generating TRN for Transaction " +
        transaction.getId() + ", device " + terminal.getId());
    String AAA = terminal.getCode();
    String YYYYMMDD = createTs();
    String counter = transactionReferenceCustomRepository.
        getCurrentCounterForDate(System.currentTimeMillis());

    String counterPadded = StringUtils.leftPad(counter, 5, "0"); //dopełniam
    String CC = securityService.generateChecksum(YYYYMMDD + counterPadded, 2);

    String trn = Joiner.on("/").join(AAA, YYYYMMDD + counterPadded, CC);
```

To move to the next occurrence of the text you are searching for, press *F3*. To get back to the previous one, press *Shift + F3*. If you are done, press the *Esc* to close the search bar.

The search functionality is available not only in the scope of the file opened in the editor, but also in the scope of a folder, module, or the whole project. In this case, the search will be called **Find In Path**. It's available in the context menu of a folder or with the *Ctrl + Shift + F* shortcut. For **Find In Path**, however, the results will be presented in a separate **Find Occurrences** tool window at the bottom of the IDE, as shown in the following screenshot:

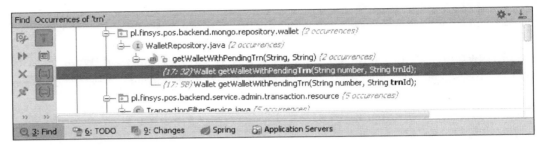

Double-clicking on the item in the list will open the file in the editor. The **Replace** functionality is very similar to **Find**. To execute **Replace** in the editor, press *Ctrl + R* (PC) or *cmd + R* (Mac):

In the Replace bar, you will have the option to restrict the replacement of text to within the selected block of code; to replace a single occurrence; or replace all of them. If you want to replace text globally in more than one file, you can also execute **Replace In Path**. It's available with the *Ctrl + Shift + F* keyboard shortcut or in the context menu of the folder in the **Project** tool window. Just like in the **Find** dialog box, you provide the scope for replacement; it can be a folder, module, or the whole project. If you accept the dialog box, IntelliJ IDEA will show the findings in the **Find Occurrences** tool window and ask if you want to replace the code occurrence, as shown in the following screenshot:

You can now perform the replacement of a single occurrence, all occurrences in this file, or all occurrences in all files.

Syntax-aware selection

The *Ctrl + W* (PC) and *cmd + W* (Mac) shortcuts will run the syntax-aware text selection. If executed for the first time, it will select the syntax block under the cursor. Every next press will expand the selection in a smart way, analyzing the source code being edited. Pressing *Ctrl + Shift + W* (PC) and *cmd + Shift + W* (Mac) will deselect the items. Context-aware selection is a very handy feature; if you get used to it, you will not use the cursor and arrow keys to select a block of code. Apart from the normal selection, you can also switch to the column selection mode.

Column selection mode

To make a selection in column selection mode, select the desired area with your mouse with the *Alt* key pressed. To toggle between the line and column selection modes permanently, pick **Column Mode** from the **Edit** menu or from the editor's context menu. Alternatively, press the *Alt + Shift + Insert* keyboard shortcut. Then, make the selection with the mouse cursor as usual:

```
}

private String createTs() {
    DateTime dt = new DateTime();
    return fmt.print(dt);
}
```

To move the selected block or just the current line up and down in the editor, use *Shift + Ctrl +* the up arrow key or down arrow key (PC) and *Shift + cmd +* the up arrow key or down arrow key (Mac).

Clipboard history

During the coding process, the clipboard is an indispensable tool. We select, cut, and copy often. Sometimes there is a need to paste the previous content of the clipboard. Press *Ctrl + Shift + V* (PC) or *cmd + Shift + V* (Mac) to display the clipboard history dialog box and select content to paste. As always, start entering search keywords to narrow the list, as shown in the following screenshot:

The clipboard history dialog box

Reformatting the code

In IntelliJ IDEA, any file, selected block of code, or all files in any directory may be formatted according to the specified code style settings. The **Code Style** section is a project-specific setting and is available in the **Code Style** section of the **Project Settings** window. There is the **General** page for general options, such as line endings and tab size. The dialog box also contains pages for other file types such as Java or SQL. The code style settings include many options, such as wrapping, braces, tabs, and indents. I believe most of the settings are very good out of the box but, if you prefer, you can tweak them to match your own code style or your organization's code style. To execute code formatting, press *Ctrl + Alt + L* (PC) or *cmd + option + L* (Mac). You can also use separate code formatting actions. To just fix the line indentations, use *Ctrl + Alt + I* (PC) or *cmd + Option + I* (Mac). Of course, standard *Tab* and *Shift + Tab* keyboard shortcuts will also work in IntelliJ IDEA. If you keep the text selected, pressing *Tab* or *Shift + Tab* will indent or unindent the selection accordingly. To clean up and organize your imports, use *Ctrl + Alt + O* (PC) or *cmd + Option + O* (Mac).

If you want to exclude a specific text block from code formatting, create formatting markers in the **General** pane of the **Project settings/Code style** dialog box. Use the **Formatter off** and **Formatter on** markers as comments to specify the code block to be excluded from formatting.

One of the newest additions to the IDE features is detecting the code style settings in the currently edited file on-the-fly. The option shown in the following screenshot is enabled by default and is available by navigating to **Settings | Editor | Code Style**:

☑ Detect and use existing file indents for editing

Having this option selected means that, even if a file has a code style different from your current settings, it will still be preserved.

Code completion

When you code, IntelliJ IDEA stands over your shoulder, watching what you are doing, and tries to help by showing hints. Sometimes the suggestion is displayed automatically without you doing anything. The methods of the specified type are displayed automatically when you put a dot after the variable name, for example. To force the hint—for example, to show the completion list for the method parameters—use the *Ctrl + Space* bar keyboard shortcut. Note that, when you press the *Tab* key to accept a completion, IntelliJ IDEA will overwrite partial expressions right to your caret. When you press *Enter* to accept a completion, IntelliJ IDEA will simply insert the completion and move everything behind the caret to make room for the completion.

```
if (device != null) {
    if (deviceValidator.validate(device, serviceReply.getErrorFields(), serviceReply.getEmptyFields())) {
        checkAndUpdatePassword(device);
        logger.info("saving device ID " + device.getId());
        devicesRepository.save();
        serviceReply.setSu  p  device                                        Device
    } else {                    f  securityService                  SecurityService
        serviceReply.setSu   m  getDevice (String id)                        Device
        serviceReply.setMe   m  getDevices ()                         List<Device>
    }                             new
}                                 null
else {
    serviceReply.setSucces  m  saveDevice (Device device)            ServiceReply
    serviceReply.setMessag  v  serviceReply                          ServiceReply
}                             m  checkAndUpdatePassword (Device device)        void
                              m  deleteDevice (Device device)                  void
Spring   Version Control
                           Dot, semicolon and some other keys will also close this lookup and be inserted into editor
```

The code completion hint

Besides using the *Ctrl* + Space Bar keyboard shortcut to get the list, you can use the Smart Type code completion feature available using the *Ctrl* + *Shift* + Space Bar keyboard shortcut. This will show a suggestion list that includes only those types that are applicable in the current code context. The Smart code completion works only in the context in which IntelliJ IDEA can determine the proper type. These contexts include the list of parameters of a method, the right part of the assignment statements, variable initializers, return statements, and the throws and new keywords, as shown in the following screenshot:

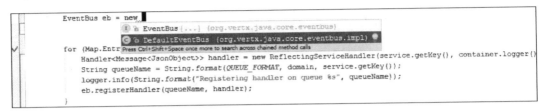

The Smart Type completion hint

> To force IntelliJ IDEA to scan even deeper and show more items on the autocomplete list, press the *Ctrl* + *Shift* + Space Bar shortcut again. IntelliJ IDEA will include the static methods that return the required type and the methods returning the collection of the desired type; you will also be able to use chained expressions. Using *Ctrl/cmd* + *Alt* + Space Bar, you can force IntelliJ IDEA to look for matches outside the currently imported classes; this is useful if you want to use a class that you haven't yet imported.

The IntelliJ IDEA code completion feature is extremely flexible. It even recognizes other languages inside string literals such as SQL assigned to String variables in the Java code and shows the code completion lists for them too.

Of course, code completion works not only in Java but in many other languages and file types, such as JavaScript, HTML, XML, CSS, Groovy, Scala, Ruby, Python, SQL, and PHP. You can also use code completion when editing resource or property files.

Code completion doesn't just work in the editor. It works in a debugger, when evaluating expressions, search inputs, and many other places in the IDE. When in doubt, try the *Ctrl* + Space Bar keyboard shortcut!

You can customize the hint settings by navigating to **Preferences / IDE / Editor / Code Completion**. You can set up various code completion options here, such as the pop-up timeout or toggle showing JavaDoc documentation. The code completion in IntelliJ IDEA is available also when you have some other language embedded in your source in the form of string literals. This feature is called language injection.

Language injection

Typical examples of the language injection are HTML fragments injected into the JavaScript code or SQL statements in Java. This feature will be active when you have the **IntelliLang** plugin enabled. The IDE will provide syntax highlighting, code completion, and hints in the scope of this string. This includes most of the supported languages, such as Java, JavaScript, Groovy, Python, Ruby, XML, and PHP. To inject the language, start typing the string expression and then press the *Alt + Enter* keyboard shortcut. Next, choose the **Inject Language/Reference** action, as shown in the following screenshot:

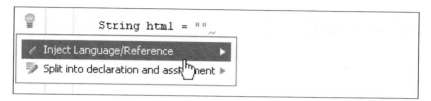

For an existing string expression, IntelliJ IDEA will try to recognize the injected language automatically. If it fails, you can use the *Alt + Enter* keyboard shortcut and again pick the **Inject Language/Reference** action. Sometimes you can help IntelliJ IDEA with the recognition process, for example, by choosing the SQL dialect, again with the *Alt + Enter* keyboard shortcut, as shown in the following screenshot:

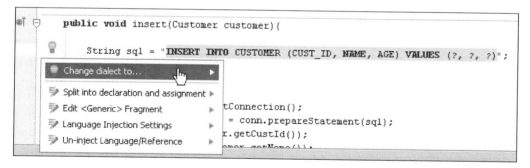

The language injection can be forced by using the @Language Java annotation or comments such as //language=<language_name>, /*language=<language_name>*/, #language=<language_name>, and <!--language=<language_name!-- >. An example is shown in the following screenshot:

```
/*#language=MySQL*/
String sql = "INSERT INTO CUSTOMER (CUST_ID, NAME, AGE) " +
             "VALUES (?, ?, ?)";
```

Generating code

Often, throughout the coding process, there are tasks that have to be done in the same way repeatedly. Generating the setters and the getter for the POJO Java class is just one example. IntelliJ IDEA supports the generation of such boilerplate coding. Press *Alt + Insert* (PC) or *Control + N* (Mac) or go to **Code | Generate** to display the **Generate** pop-up:

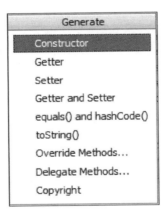

After picking the desired code block to be generated, the next pop-up will be shown with the selection of properties that should be used to generate this block. Select the properties and watch the boilerplate code generate automatically in the editor. Apart from just generating simple code snippets, Generate can also guess what should be added to the constructor by looking at the class, finding defined variables, and proposing to add them as constructor parameters, which really makes this feature powerful. Code generation can save a lot of development time everyday.

Code inspection

IntelliJ IDEA's editor can show not only compiler errors, but also compliance with the coding guidelines and standards, dead code, probable bugs, performance issues, and conformity to specifications, such as Struts, JSF, EJB, and many others. The analysis of the source code is performed as you type, so no additional action is required for the feature to run, but it can be forced by using **Inspect Code** from the **Analyze** menu. The result of the analysis will be presented in the **Inspection Results** tool window:

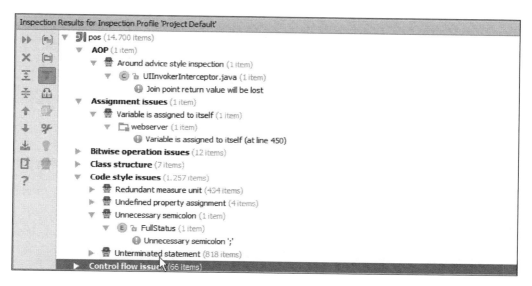

Clicking on an item in the list will open the specific file in the editor. If it might be possible to automatically fix the issue found, IntelliJ IDEA will present a yellow bulb icon; this denotes a quick fix hint, as shown in the following screenshot:

```
private Handler<Message<JsonObject>> loginHandler;
private Handler<Message<JsonObject>> logoutHandler;
private Handler<Message<JsonO
                              Field can be converted to a local variable more... (Ctrl+F1)
```

If the quick fix icon is displayed, the keyboard shortcut *Alt + Enter* will list the possible actions that can be taken to eliminate the issue. Select the action of your choice. Most of the time, issues will be fixed automatically. *Alt + Enter* is probably one of the most important shortcuts you need to know in IntelliJ IDEA. Basically, if used correctly, you can get a ton of productivity with it. It can also be applied to code that is not actually marked as an error. If you use it, IntelliJ IDEA will analyze the context you are in and propose to perform quick tasks, such as creating a subclass, adding getters and setters, assigning constructor parameters to variables, adding casts, using static import instead of a fully qualified name, autogeneration of variable assignments (if executed at the beginning of a line, which would evaluate to a value), and so on, all with the same keystroke—*Alt + Enter*.

Experiment with *Alt + Enter* while using the editor to see which tasks are possible. It's a huge time-saver.

As you can see by now, the editor in IntelliJ is very powerful and equipped with many productivity shortcuts. However, there's more: Live Templates and postfix completion.

Using Live Templates

Live Templates lets you use the editor to insert frequently used code blocks into your source code.

Live Templates can be simple, parameterized, and surrounded. A simple template contains code blocks that will be expanded and inserted into the editor, replacing the abbreviation. Parameterized templates, on the other hand, have variables that will be filled automatically by IntelliJ IDEA or will prompt the user for input.

When a parameterized template is invoked and expanded in the editor, IntelliJ IDEA will suggest some predefined values for the defined variables. The surrounding templates expand before and after the selected code block. To insert a live template into the editor, just type the abbreviation and press the expand key (*Tab* is the default key). The other way to insert a template is to press *Ctrl + J* (PC) or *cmd + J* (Mac) and select the template from the pop-up list. As always, you can filter the list by typing.

The pop-up list will contain Live Templates that can be applied in the current context. The context is related to the file type you edit (Java or HTML, for example) and also to the code block you are in, such as a method or field declaration. The templates are context-aware; IntelliJ IDEA will try to autocomplete the sections of the template, based on the current context.

```
private Object[] getParameterValues(JsonObject request, Method resourcMethod) throws IOException {
    Annotation[][] parameterAnnotations = resourcMethod.getParameterAnnotations();
    Class[] parameterTypes = resourcMethod.getParameterTypes();
    Object[] paramValues = new Object[parameterTypes.length];

    int i = 0;

    for (int j = 0; j < paramValues.length; j++) {
        = paramVa  v o paramValues              Object[]
                   v o parameterTypes            Class[]
                   v o parameterAnnotations      Annotation[][]
    for (Annotation[] annotations : parameterAnnotations) {
        int index = i++;
        Class parameterType = parameterTypes[index];
```

Executing a parameterized live template

The surrounding live templates are executed by using the *Ctrl + Alt + J* (PC) or *cmd + Option + J* (Mac) keyboard shortcut. Select the text you want to execute a template with, hit the keyboard shortcut, and you are done. The surrounding template isn't any different from the normal templates, besides the fact that the chosen block of code (or text) is assigned to the $SELECTION$ variable, as shown in the following screenshot:

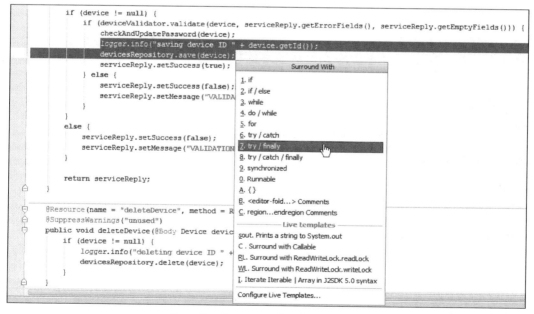

Executing the surrounding live template

IntelliJ IDEA has many inbuilt templates out of the box; you can use them after installing the IDE. You can also create your own live templates. To do this, go to **IDE Settings | Live Templates** in the **Settings** dialog box.

Feel free to browse and look into the existing templates to get familiar with the syntax.

To add a new template, select the green **+** icon on the right-hand side of the window, as shown in the following screenshot:

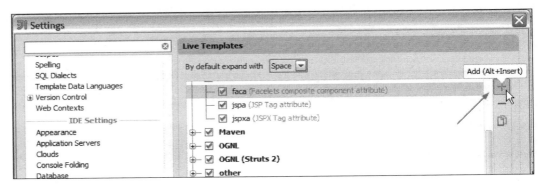

Adding a new live template

The template definition consists of the abbreviation, the actual template text, the variables, and the context this template should be recognized in.

The context will be a development language such as Java, for example, and a syntax element such as a declaration or expression, for example.

Variable names begin and end with the dollar sign. There are two predefined variables available. The END variable is where the cursor will be when the template expands and the $SELECTION$ variable mentioned earlier represents the selected text in the case of surrounding templates.

If the template contains the $SELECTION$ variable, it will become a surrounding template and will be available with the surrounding template keyboard shortcut. Also, this kind of template will not appear in the list of normal templates provided via *Ctrl + J* (PC) or *cmd + J* (Mac).

When defining a template, you can use these two predefined variables or define your own. If you decide to use your own variable, just type its name with dollar signs in the template body. The **Edit variables** button will become active, allowing you to define this custom variable. The variable editor allows you to enter an expression, which can be a function, and the default value. Refer to the documentation for the list of supported functions.

You can even execute Groovy scripts as the expression. This is a powerful feature with almost endless possibilities! You can try to change the Live Template expansion shortcut key from the *Tab* key, which is set by default to *Space Bar*. You may find it more natural to expand live templates using the Space Bar.

Live Templates is a mighty feature. If you memorize the abbreviations for the templates you use the most, your coding speed will be unbeaten. A feature somewhat related to the live templates is postfix completion.

Postfix code completion

Postfix code completion lets you transform an already typed expression into another one. This can be explained by the following example. Let's use the `.format` postfix completion. If you type `"myString".format` and then press *Tab*, the code will get wrapped into `String.format("myString").` automatically. Postfix completions just like Live Templates can be of the neighboring type. For example, the `.notnull` postfix completion will wrap the expression with the null value checking code block.

You can see all defined postfix templates and disable the ones you don't want by navigating to **Settings | Editor | General | Postfix Completion**, as shown in the following screenshot:

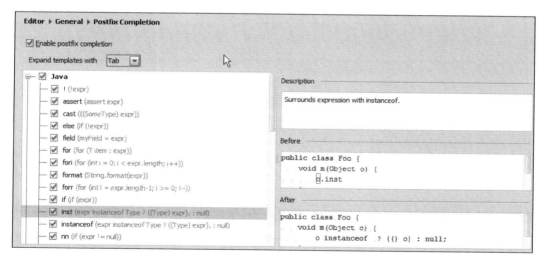

Although you cannot define your own postfix completion templates, the provided set for Java and JavaScript is more than enough to dramatically improve the speed of the development process. Combined with Live Templates, postfix code completion is a very powerful editor feature.

We already know a lot about editing code in IntelliJ IDEA. In the next section, you will learn how to compare files and folders.

Comparing files and folders

When you develop a project, often there is a need to compare the contents of the files or the structures of the folders. Usually, you would have to use an external tool for that, and there are plenty of such tools in the market. IntelliJ IDEA provides its own file diff and folder synchronization features. Let's start with comparing files.

Comparing files

To compare two files, select them keeping the *Ctrl* key pressed in the project structure tree and choose **Compare Two Files** from the context menu; or press *Ctrl + D* (PC) or *cmd + D* (Mac). The differences viewer will open with the differences highlighted:

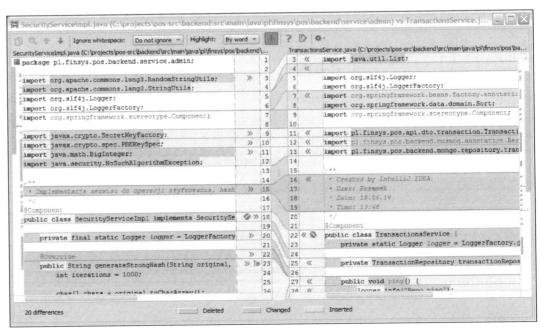

You can move between code differences using the arrows in the differences viewer toolbar or by pressing the keyboard shortcuts; *F7* will jump to the next difference and *Shift + F7* to the previous one.

To synchronize two files, use the "Replace" arrow buttons in the middle of the editor. To move the change from the left file to the right one, press the **>>** icon. To move from right to left, use the **<<** icon. Every difference block has a context menu available, where you can select the whole modified block. You can replace, insert, or remove the change, as shown in the following screenshot:

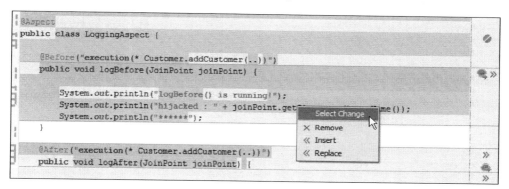

Take note that the contents shown in the diff editor are syntax-highlighted and still have a gutter area and stripe marks on the scroll area. On the status bar of the diff editor, the information about the number of remaining differences is displayed, as shown in the following screenshot:

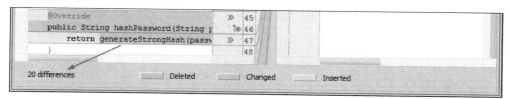

The number of differences

The differences viewer can also compare the current editor contents with the contents of the clipboard. Just right-click inside the editor area and choose **Compare with Clipboard**.

 You can also compare images using the differences viewer.

Comparing folders

To compare two folders, select them in the project tree with the *Ctrl* key pressed and, again, use *Ctrl + D* (PC) or *cmd + D* (Mac). The folder directory diff window will open, displaying the differences between the chosen folders, as shown in the following screenshot:

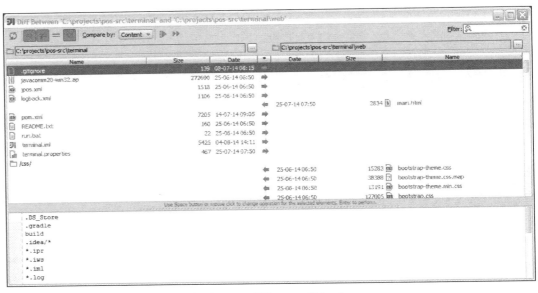

The directory differences dialog box

In the upper toolbar, you can filter the file list contents to display new files on the left side, new files on the right side, different files on both sides, and equal files on the both sides.

At the bottom of the directory differences viewer, there is a regular diff viewer pane, showing the detailed breakdown of differences of the selected files, the same as when comparing files.

Use the arrows in the middle section of the diff viewer to mark the files to be copied from the left to right, right to left, or deleted if non-existent in one of the directories. Pressing *Enter* will synchronize the selected files, and pressing *Ctrl + Enter* (PC) or *cmd + Enter* (Mac) will synchronize all files.

From now on, you will not need an external tool to see the differences and synchronize files and directories. Let's summarize the keyboard shortcuts you learned so far.

The following table summarizes basic editor commands:

Action	PC shortcut	Mac shortcut
Duplicating the line or selected block	Ctrl + D	cmd + D
Deleting the line or selected block	Ctrl + Y	cmd + Y
Line comment	Ctrl + /	cmd + /
Block comment	Shift + Ctrl + /	Shift + cmd + /
Joining lines	Shift + Ctrl + J	Shift + Ctrl + J
Toggle case	Shift + Ctrl + U	Shift + cmd + U
Find	Ctrl + F	cmd + F
Find In Path	Shift + Ctrl + F	Shift + Ctrl + F
Replace	Ctrl + R	cmd + R
Replace In Path	Shift + Ctrl + R	Shift + Ctrl + R
Reformatting code	Ctrl + Alt + L	cmd + option + L
Automatically indenting lines	Ctrl + Alt + I	cmd + option + I
Indenting a selection	Tab	Tab
Unindenting a selection	Shift + Tab	Shift + Tab
Optimizing imports	Ctrl + Alt + O	cmd + option + O
Executing the Live Template	Ctrl + J	cmd + J
Executing the surrounding Live Template	Ctrl + Alt + J	cmd + option + J
Showing the intention pop/up	Alt + Enter	Alt + Enter
Showing the code completion pop/up	Ctrl + Space Bar	control + Space Bar
Generating code	Alt + Insert	control + N
Comparing files or folders	Ctrl + D	cmd + D

Looking for help

During the coding process, it's convenient to have the code documentation close at hand. IntelliJ IDEA can extract the documentation straight from the source (using JavaDoc) or display the external documentation.

Viewing inline documentation

To view inline documentation, use **Quick Documentation Lookup**, which is available with *Ctrl + Q* (PC) or *control + J* (Mac). The dialog box will display the documentation for the symbol or method under the cursor, but only if the symbol or method has been provided with documentation comments. You can go through the quick documentation using the provided hyperlinks and arrow buttons to move back and forth through the pages. The **Quick Documentation Lookup** window can be pinned to become a tool window (we described this in the first chapter), as shown in the following screenshot:

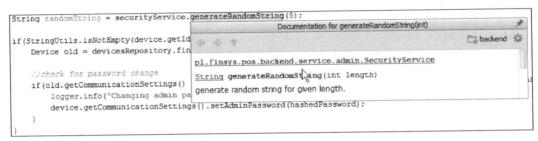

Quick documentation lookup

 For markup languages, IntelliJ IDEA will show the documentation extracted from a document definition file such as DTD or XML Schema.

Viewing type definitions

To look at the implementation of the symbol at the cursor, execute the quick definition pop-up by pressing *Shift + Ctrl + I* (PC) or *cmd + Y* (Mac). IntelliJ IDEA will display the source code fragment with the definition of the symbol. It can be the type, variable, or method as shown in the following screenshot:

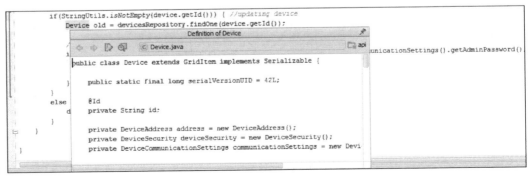

The quick definition pop-up

Looking for usages

The **Show Usages** feature is a very handy feature that will display the usages for any symbol under the cursor. Execute an action using *Alt + Ctrl + F7* (PC) or *cmd + Alt + F7* (Mac):

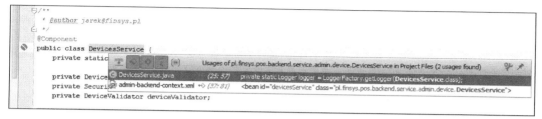

The Show Usages pop up

You can also use *Alt + F7* (in both PC and Mac) if you want to have the usages in an extra **Find Usages** tool window for later reference.

> **Quick Documentation Lookup**, **Quick Definition**, and **Show Usages** pop-up windows also work in the code completion lists. When choosing a method from the code completion list, for example, just press the corresponding shortcut to display the documentation. It works even for the elements in the navigation bar we discussed earlier.

Viewing method parameters

To view the method parameter information, press *Ctrl + P* or *cmd + P* (Mac). IDEA will display the pop up with the required parameters, extracted from the source code:

```
//check for password change
if(old.getCommunicationSettings() == null || !StringUtils.equals(old.getCommunicationSettings()
    logger.info("Changing admin password for the device " + device.getId());
    device.getCommunicationSettings().setAdminPassword(hashedPassword);
}
}
                                        String adminPassword
```

Viewing parameter information

Viewing the external documentation

If the documentation is long and more detailed, it may be more convenient to display it in the external browser, outside the IDE. To do this, use the *Shift + F1* keyboard shortcut or the **View/External documentation** menu option.

Take note that the paths to the external documentation have to be properly defined in the **Project structure** dialog box. To add documentation for a module, select the module in the **Modules** section, and click on the globe icon in the JavaDoc pane, as shown in the following screenshot:

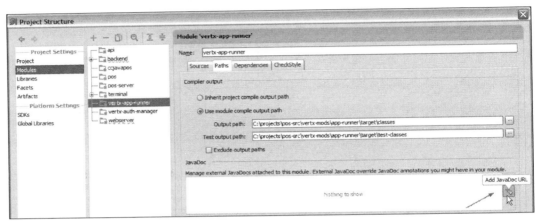

Adding external documentation for a module

To set up the external documentation for a library, select the library from the **Libraries** section and click on the same globe icon:

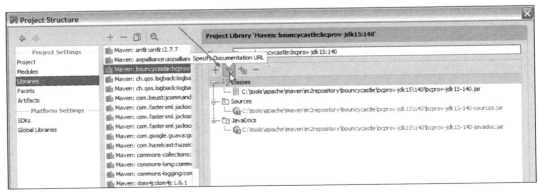

Adding external documentation for a library

IntelliJ IDEA provides a number of ways to display the documentation. The following table summarizes the keyboard shortcuts for them:

Action	PC shortcut	Mac shortcut
Quick documentation lookup	*Ctrl + Q*	*control + J*
Quick definition	*Shift + Ctrl + I*	*cmd + Y*
Show usages	*Alt + Ctrl + F7*	*cmd + Alt + F7*
Parameter info	*Ctrl + P*	*cmd + P*
External documentation	*Shift + F1*	*Shift + F1*

Summary

This was a long chapter. After all, the editor is the main functionality of the IDE. You learned how to quickly navigate across many files in a project and within a single file as well. You are now able to use and define live templates, compare files and folders, and look for the documentation. In the next chapter, we will focus on refactoring—a powerful technique to improve the source code and see how IntelliJ IDEA supports this feature.

4
Make It Better – Refactoring

In this chapter, we will take a look at source code refactoring in IntelliJ IDEA. Refactoring is the process of restructuring your source code base without changing its behavior. It enhances code readability and reduces its complexity. When the internal code structure improves, the code becomes easier to maintain and extend. Refactoring is important not only during everyday work on your own code, but for legacy code as well. The refactoring patterns are catalogued by Martin Fowler at www.refactoring.com. This is a great resource — the catalogue contains a detailed description of each refactoring along with the corresponding code example. We will focus on how IntelliJ IDEA helps with executing these refactoring actions.

We will cover the following topics in this chapter:

- An overview of refactoring
- The most important refactoring actions
- A summary of refactoring shortcuts

With every new release, IntelliJ IDEA contains additional refactoring actions, so the arsenal grows. Let's take a look at the refactoring process now.

An overview of refactoring

IntelliJ IDEA offers an impressive set of code refactoring actions. The good thing is that the refactoring process in IntelliJ IDEA is not limited purely to the Java language. If you have installed the corresponding plugins, refactoring will be available for other languages and frameworks as well. This includes SQL expressions, database table definitions, Spring annotations, expressions, configurations, Hibernate mappings, JSF expressions, and so on.

To start refactoring, you will first have to select the code fragment that you want to refactor; we will call it the refactoring target. This can be a symbol or just a piece of code. The symbol can be selected in the editor; it is usually sufficient to have the caret on the symbol that you want to refactor. IntelliJ IDEA will expand the selection automatically. This is quite a time saver. You can also pick the symbol in the **Project** view, **Structure** tool window, or the **Commander** tool window, if you have the **Commander** plugin installed.

 In the Ultimate edition, if you have the UML plugin installed, you can select the target in the UML Class diagram.

Having selected your target, pick the desired refactoring action. All of them are available in the **Refactor** menu item, or in the context menu that we get by clicking on the right mouse button, as shown in the following screenshot:

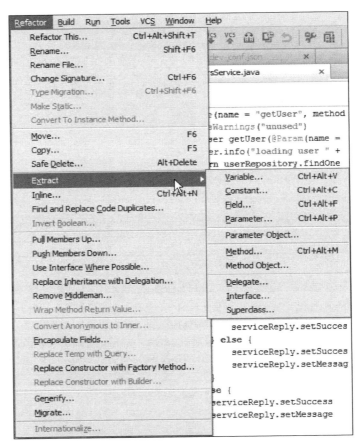

As always, it's a lot more convenient to use keyboard shortcuts to pick refactoring actions. Try to memorize the ones you use the most or pick the first option **Refactor This...** from the menu, the result of which is shown in the following screenshot:

```
@Resource(name = "processElectricityBillTrn", method = Resource.Method.POST)
public ElectricityBillTrnDTO processElectricityBillTrn(@Body ElectricityBillTrnDTO transaction) {
    logger.info("Recived transaction to process: " + transaction.toString());
    transaction.setIsCrt                 Refactor This
    transactionReposi
    return transaction;      1. Rename...
}                            2. Change Signature...
                             3. Make Static...
@Resource(name = "proces                          .Method.POST)
public WaterBillTrnDTO p     4. Move...               lTrnDTO transaction) {
    logger.info("Recived     5. Copy...               saction.toString());
    transaction.setTsCrt     6. Safe Delete...
    transactionRepositor     ──────── Extract ────────
    return transaction;      7. Variable...
}                            8. Constant...
                             9. Field...
@Resource(name = "valida     0. Parameter...          .Method.POST)
public PhoneNumberValida     Parameter Object...      @Body PhoneNumberValidationRequest request)
    logger.info("Validat     Method...                oneNumber());
    PhoneNumberValidatio     Method Object...         lidationResponse();
    res.setValid(!"00000     Delegate...              )));
    logger.info("Phone n     Interface...             + " valid "+res.isValid());
    return res;              Superclass...
}
                             Inline...
```

The Refactor This... pop-up menu

Use the *Ctrl + Shift + Alt + T* (PC) or *control + T* (Mac) keyboard shortcut to display the pop-up menu with refactoring actions available in the current context.

Refactoring works together with code analysis; it uses the index that IntelliJ IDEA built during code scanning. This is the reason why most refactorings are disabled when IntelliJ IDEA updates its indexes. Naturally, not all of the refactoring actions are available for all of the chosen targets. For example, you cannot pull a class member up if the class doesn't have the superclass or interface it implements.

When you choose any of the refactoring actions, IntelliJ IDEA will analyze the selected target to check whether the chosen action is possible in the current context. If the refactoring action is not possible, IntelliJ IDEA will prompt that it cannot be done, giving detailed information about the reason, as shown in the following screenshot:

```
@Resource(name = "getUser", method = Resource.Method.GET)
@SuppressWarnings (     Cannot perform refactoring.
public User getUse    pl.finsys.UsersService does not have base classes/interfaces in current project
    logger.info("loading user" + id);
    return userRepository.findByIdAndActive(id, Boolean.TRUE);
}
```

On the other hand, if refactoring is possible, most of the time you will be presented with a supplementary action-specific dialog box with refactoring options.

For certain types of refactoring, the IDE will give you the possibility to preview the scope of the changes to be made. In the **Find Refactoring Preview** tool window, IntelliJ IDEA will list the references that will be changed. You can right-click on a single item or the whole subtree in the list and exclude it from the refactoring process, as shown in the following screenshot:

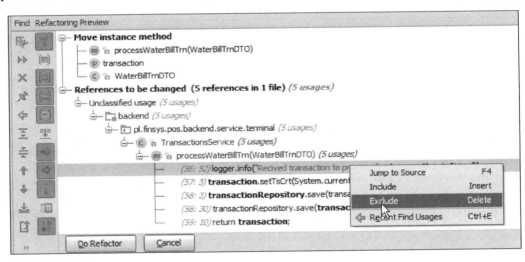

To execute refactoring, select the **Do Refactor** button. To cancel the process, just hit **Cancel**.

If IntelliJ IDEA detects that a certain action can cause problems in the source, it will show the **Problems Detected** dialog box, giving you a detailed description of the problem, as shown in the following screenshot:

You can now list the problems in a separate tool window by clicking on the **Show conflicts in view** button. This will allow you to investigate the problems found, exclude some of the changes, cancel the action, or force to do it anyway, as shown in the following screenshot:

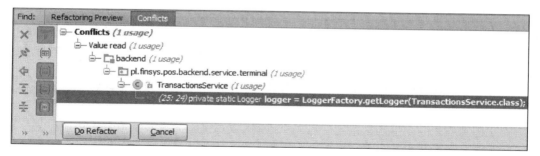

Depending on the refactoring action chosen, IntelliJ IDEA can display in-place suggestions in the refactoring prompt. For example, if you decide to execute the *Rename* refactoring action, use the corresponding shortcut (*Shift + F6* in this case) and IntelliJ IDEA will suggest some new names for you, as shown in the following screenshot:

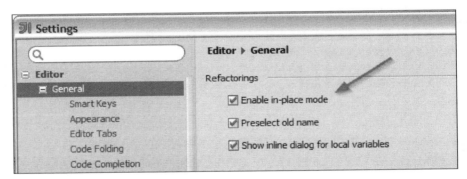

If you use the shortcut again, instead of the in-place prompt, the refactoring options dialog box will be shown. If you don't like the in-place refactoring options and prefer to see the dialog box always, the in-place mode can be switched off in the **Settings** window in the **Editor | General** section, as shown in the following screenshot:

Don't be afraid to mess up your code. You can always revert the refactoring, using **Undo** from the **Edit** menu, or by using the *Ctrl + Z* (PC) or *cmd + Z* (Mac) shortcut. It also never hurts to have a version control system for your project.

Now we know how to select the refactoring target and execute the refactoring actions. Let's take a look at some of the important and useful refactoring actions available.

Refactoring actions

There are many different refactoring actions available in IntelliJ IDEA. Let's cover the important ones first: **Rename, Copy, Move,** and **Safe Delete.**

Rename

This is probably the most commonly used refactoring. The target for the rename action can be any symbol in the source code: class, method, field, method parameter, or local variable.

To rename, just pick the target and press *Shift + F6*. This action will start the in-place prompt, as shown in the following screenshot:

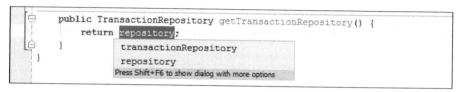

If you use the *Shift + F6* shortcut twice, the **Rename** dialog box will offer additional options such as searching within comments and text strings, as shown here:

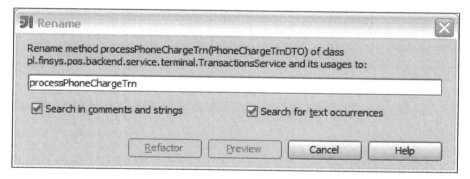

IntelliJ IDEA handles renaming intelligently; it will offer to rename the getter and setter methods if any of them are found. If the target to be renamed is the name of a type, the IDE will offer to rename variables of that type, the inheritors, implementing classes, and corresponding tests.

Find and Replace Code Duplicates

According to the **don't repeat yourself (DRY)** principle, you should avoid code duplication. **Find and Replace Code Duplication** refactoring will search code duplicates for the designated target. First, pick the scope for the duplicates search; it can be the whole project, a selected module, uncommitted files, or just the current file, as shown in the following screenshot:

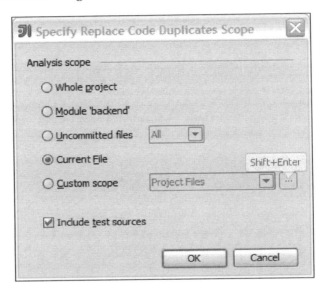

When a duplicate is found, IntelliJ IDEA will show the dialog box with the option to replace or skip the occurrence, as shown in the following screenshot:

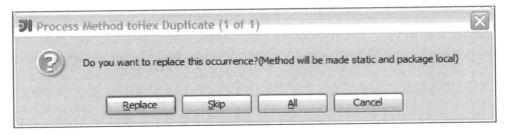

Copy

The **Copy** refactoring allows you to make a copy of the class selected as the target. It can be copied into the same package or a new package. The copy will be opened in the editor, by default. In the dialog box, enter the new name of the class and, optionally, a different package or directory, as shown here:

 You can execute the **Copy** refactoring by applying your OS copy and paste commands (*Ctrl + C* or *Ctrl + V* on PC and *cmd + C / cmd + V* on MAC) to the project tree. You can also use the default copy shortcut copy, which is *F5*.

Move

If used on a class, **Move** refactoring is similar to the **Copy** refactoring but will move the selected target to the new package or directory instead of copying it. The default shortcut for the **Move** operation is *F6*.

Move refactoring can also be used to move the static members of a class or static methods to an other class. In this case, the dialog box will ask for the destination class and present its visibility pane to give you the opportunity to change the visibility of the property or method being moved, as shown here:

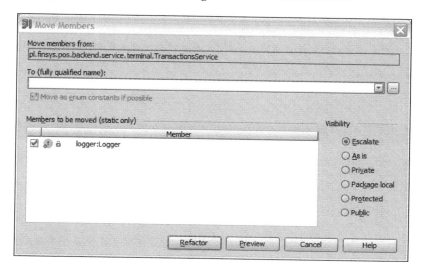

The **To (fully qualified name)** field has somewhat similar behavior to a standard editor (it performs code completion so you don't have to type the fully classified name but just the class name; IntelliJ IDEA will offer a list of proposed classes). Additionally, if you type the name of a class that doesn't exist yet, IntelliJ IDEA will propose to create it. The **Choose Destination Class** window allows you to not only change the target package/directory but also the source root (for example, to move a class from the main tree to the test tree), as shown here:

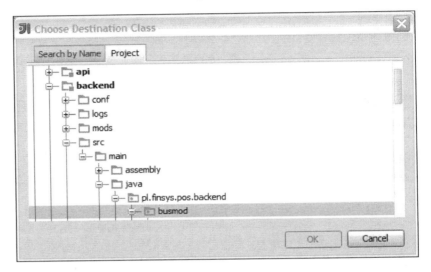

 You can execute **Move** refactoring by dragging the class to the other package in the project tree.

You can also execute **Move** refactoring on the whole package. In this case, IntelliJ IDEA will ask what your intentions are; you can just move the package or the directory to another source root or move everything to another directory, as shown here:

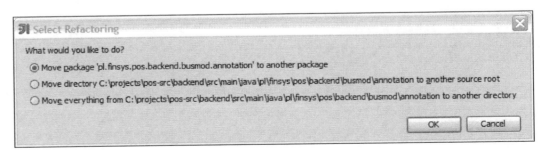

Move Instance Method

If you decide to execute Move refactoring on the method that is not static, it will become **Move Instance Method** refactoring. Move Instance Method is not available as a separate item in the **Refactor** menu. IntelliJ IDEA detects that the method you want to move is the instance method and will present a dialog box to select an instance parameter and visibility, as shown here:

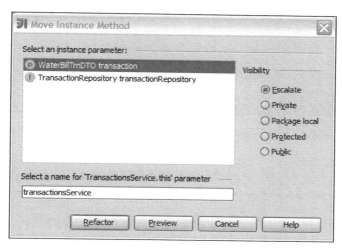

Safe Delete

The target for delete refactoring can be a class, interface, method, field, or parameter. IntelliJ IDEA will find all the usages of the specified target within the whole project. If the object you want to delete is not being used anywhere, IntelliJ IDEA will just silently remove it. On the other hand, if the object is being referenced somewhere else in the project, the usages will be presented in the **Find usages** tool window. You can inspect the usages and force the deletion from here:

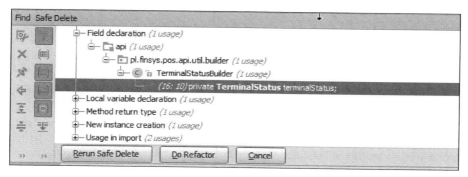

You can execute **Find Safe Delete** by selecting the class in the project tree and using the *Alt + Delete* (PC) or *cmd + delete* (MAC) keyboard shortcut.

Change Signature

Use this action to change the signature of a method. You can change a method's visibility, name, number of parameters and their types and order, the returned type, and a list of exceptions the method throws. The default shortcut for **Change Signature** is *Ctrl + F6* (PC) or *cmd + F6* (Mac).

When changing the parameter's type, IntelliJ IDEA will show a list containing the types found in the current project. Just start entering text to narrow the list down.

At the bottom of the dialog box, there is a rendered preview of what the method signature would look like after performing the action, as shown in the following screenshot:

The standard shortcuts (*Alt + Insert, Alt + Delete, Alt +* the up arrow key, and *Alt +* the down arrow key) can be used to insert, delete, move up, and move down parameters respectively.

Type Migration

Use the **Type Migration** feature to change the type of the symbol, for example, from `String` to `Integer`. The symbol can be a method parameter or class member. This feature is really powerful and allows changing all the code related to the changed symbol to accommodate that type of migration. Select the type you want to migrate and execute the action. The standard shortcut for this is *Ctrl + Shift + F6* (PC) or *cmd + Shift + F6* (Mac). IntelliJ IDEA will show a dialog box with a drop-down list of types available, as shown in the following screenshot:

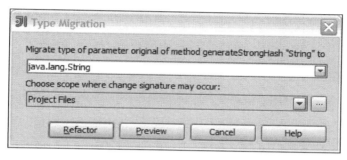

Make Static

The Make Static refactoring can be used to convert a method from being an instance method to a static method. If you select **Add object as a parameter with name**, IntelliJ IDEA will create the static method with a parameter of the same type as the method's origin class. If you refactor a method, there is also an option to create a parameter for fields that are referenced from that method instead of passing the whole object instance.

 Be cautious about converting a method so it's static. It's not considered a good practice to have a static method that changes state.

Convert to Instance Method

This action is the opposite of **Make static**. Use the action to turn a static method into a class instance method. The type of the static method parameter will be picked by IntelliJ IDEA as the target class for the method. You will be asked whether the visibility of the new method is public, protected, or private.

Extract refactorings

The largest group of refactoring actions is the Extract group. They are very useful when restructuring code. If IntelliJ IDEA detects multiple occurrences of the selected refactoring target, it will offer the option to replace all the found occurrences. Let's take a look at extract refactorings in detail.

Extract Variable

Extract Variable refactoring, executed with *Ctrl + Alt + V* (PC) or *cmd + option + V* (Mac), will turn the target—the expression selected in the editor—into a variable. The type of the new variable will be the same type as returned by the expression. IntelliJ IDEA will propose some meaningful names for the variable to choose from. If you don't select an expression but just have your caret over one, IntelliJ will ask you which part of the expression should be converted into a variable. Also, if your code contains a similar expression to the one that you just converted to a variable, then IntelliJ will offer to use the newly introduced variable. Additionally, you can declare the variable as final, as shown here:

```
        char[] chars = original.toCharArray();
        try {
            byte[] sal          tBytes();
                        Declare final
            PBEKeySpec spec = new PBEKeySpec(chars, saltArr, iterations, 64 * 8);
            SecretKeyFactory pbkdf2WithHmacSHA1 = SecretKeyFactory.getInstance("PBKDF2WithHmacSHA1");
            SecretKeyFactory skf = pbkdf2WithHmacSHA1;
            byte[] hash = skf.generateSecret(spec).getEncoded();
            return toHex(hash);
        } catch (Exception e) {
            logger.error(e.getMessage(), e);
            return original;
        }
    }
```

Extract Constant

This refactoring is similar to the **Extract Variable** refactoring, but this time the target is a code block that can be represented as a constant variable; a number or string, for example. Again, IntelliJ IDEA will present you with some names to choose from. You can move the constant variable to another class if you wish to, by selecting the checkbox in the pop up, as shown in the next screenshot:

```
    char[] chars = original.toCharArray();
    try {
        byte[] saltAr
```
```
        public static final String PBKDF_2_WITH_HMAC_SHA_1 = "PBKDF2WithHmacSHA1";
        ☐ Move to another class
```
```
    PBEKeySpec spec = new PBEKeySpec(chars, saltArr, it.ations, 64 * 8);
    SecretKeyFactory skf = SecretKeyFactory.getInstance( PBKDF_2_WITH_HMAC_SHA_1 );
        byte[] hash = skf.generateSecret(spec).getEncoded()   PBKDF_2_WITH_HMAC_SHA_1
        return toHex(hash);                                    WITH_HMAC_SHA_1
    } catch (Exception e) {                                    HMAC_SHA_1
        Logger.error(e.getMessage(), e);                       SHA_1
        return original;                                       PBKDF2_WITH_HMAC_SHA1
    }                                                          STRING
}                                                              Press Ctrl+Alt+C to show dialog with more options
```

In IntelliJ IDEA, pop-ups usually have these checkboxes with the standard
Alt + *<UnderscoredLetter>* shortcuts available. In our preceding example,
this would be *Alt* + *M*.

Execute **Extract Constant** by using the *Ctrl* + *Alt* + *C* (PC) or *cmd* + *option* + *C*
(Mac) keyboard shortcut.

Extract Field

The target for **Extract Field** refactoring could be the local variable or expression.
Execute **Extract Field** refactoring with *Ctrl* + *Alt* + *F* (PC) or *cmd* + *option* + *F* (Mac).
The selection will be transformed to the class field and then initialized. All the
references to the selection will be replaced by the field usage. IntelliJ IDEA will ask
for the place you want to initialize the variable in. It can be the current method, field
declaration, or constructor of the class. If there is no constructor defined in the class,
it will be generated for you, as shown here:

```
    char[] chars = original.toCharArray();
    try {
        byte[] saltArr = salt.getBytes();        private String pbkdf2WithHmacSHA1;

                                                 Initialize in: current method
    PBEKeySpec spec = new PBEKeySpec(chars, sal        current method    s, 64 * 8);
    SecretKeyFactory skf = SecretKeyFactory.get        field declaration    WithHmacSHA1);
        byte[] hash = skf.generateSecret(spec).getE    constructor
        return toHex(hash);
    } catch (Exception e) {
        Logger.error(e.getMessage(), e);
        return original;
    }
}
```

If you execute **Extract Field** refactoring in the test class, you will have the chance
to initialize the variable in the `setUp` method as well.

Extract Parameter

If you use the *Ctrl + Alt + P* (PC) or *cmd + option + P* (Mac) shortcut, Extract Parameter method refactoring will transform the selected expression or field into the method parameter. When the method in which the new parameter is introduced is one of the inherited ones, IntelliJ IDEA will display a pop-up where you confirm the method you would like to place the new parameter in. This has been shown in the following screenshot:

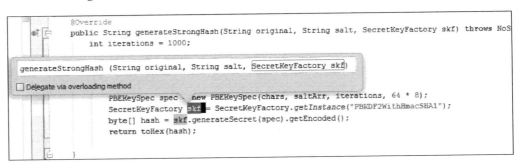

IntelliJ IDEA will then scan for usages of the method and present a second dialog box where you can delegate the method call via the overloading method, as shown in the following screenshot:

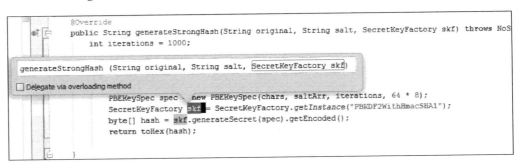

If you press the keyboard shortcut again, you'll be shown a dialog box with more advanced options.

Introduce Parameter Object

When a method has a large number of parameters, it is a good idea to encapsulate them into a wrapper — parameter object. It will be easier to modify the list of parameters later, especially where there is a chain of delegating method calls.

In the **Introduce Parameter Object** dialog box, you will have the choice to create a new wrapper class or use the existing class. All of the method parameters will be selected by default, but you can amend the list by checking the appropriate checkboxes as shown here:

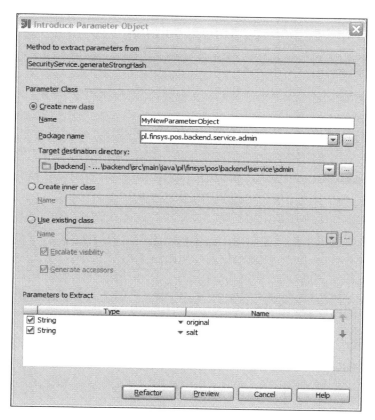

Extract Method

Extract method — executed with *Ctrl + Alt + M* (PC) or *cmd + option + M* (Mac) — will turn a selected block of code into a method and place a call to this method in place of the selected block. This can be useful when the body of your method is long and complicated and needs to be broken down into smaller pieces. Duplicated code fragments are the best candidates to be extracted as a method.

Variables used in the selection will be analyzed and proposed as a method's input parameters. This action is opposite to **Inline method**, which we will describe in a while. In the dialog box, you provide the method's name. IntelliJ IDEA will suggest parameter names and their order, but you can change them at will. As with **Change Signature** refactoring, there is a preview of the new method's signature available, as shown in the following screenshot:

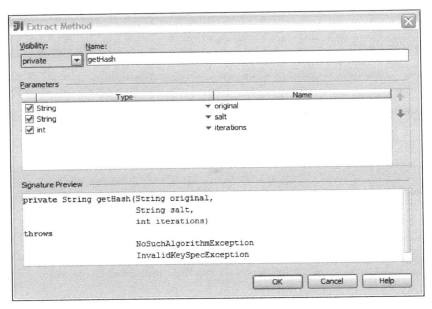

The Extract Method object

This is the alternative action for **Extract Method** and can be used when the method has multiple return values. The extracted method will be placed in the new object; it can be the inner or anonymous class. The local variables in the method will be converted into fields of the new class being created. Consider the following code example (made to be readable). Before the refactoring, we create a method that computes something and returns multiple values:

```
private int calculate (int one, int two, int three) {
  if (three == 0) {
    return 0;
  }
  else {
    return one + two;
  }
}
```

After extracting the method object from the method's body, the new class is created as shown in the following code snippet:

```
private class Calculator {
  private int one;
  private int two;
  private int three;

  public Calculator(int one, int two, int three) {
    this.one = one;
    this.two = two;
    this.three = three;
  }

  public int invoke() {
    if (three == 0) {
      return 0;
    }
    else {
      return one + two;
    }
  }
}
```

The call will be a lot cleaner with just one return point:

```
private int calculate (int one, int two, int three) {
  return new Calculator(one, two, three).invoke();
}
```

Delegate

Delegate is **Extract Class** refactoring. You have probably heard about the single responsibility principle—S in the SOLID principles. The SOLID principles were proposed by Robert C. Martin (Uncle Bob). They contain five basic principles of object-oriented programming and design. You can read more about them at `http://butunclebob.com/ArticleS.UncleBob.PrinciplesOfOod`. One of the principles is that every class should have only one responsibility. Delegate comes in handy when you need to extract members (fields and methods) to a new class, thus reducing the responsibility of the original class.

In the following dialog box, specify a name and package for the new class and select members to extract with their visibility. If you check the **Generate accessors** checkbox, setter and getter methods will be generated for the extracted:

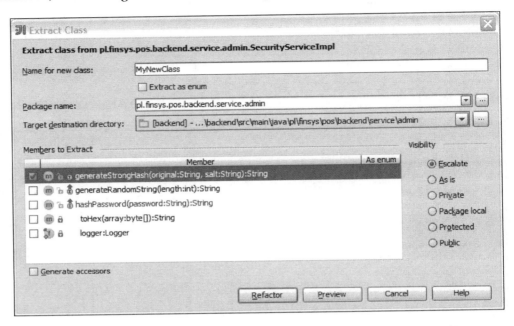

As a result of the refactoring action, IntelliJ IDEA will create a new class, instantiate it in the original class, and then delegate all the required method calls to the new class. **Delegate** is the opposite of the **Remove Middleman** refactoring we will see in a while.

Extract Interface

The **Extract Interface** refactoring creates an interface from the selected class. The class will be changed to implement this new interface. There are two options here. You can just extract the interface by providing its name and selecting the methods and static fields for extraction. You can also rename the original class, so the name of the interface will be the same as the class name previously. IntelliJ IDEA will then scan for its usages and try to use the new interface where possible. The scan results will be presented in the **Preview** tool window, where you can review the changes and approve or reject them, as shown in the following screenshot:

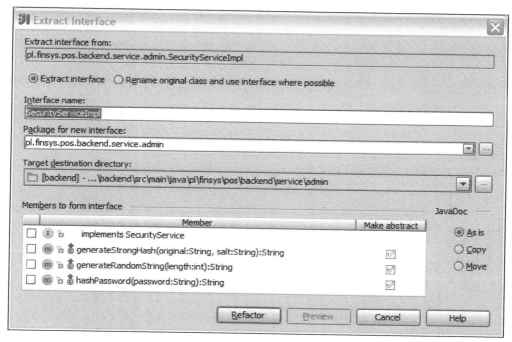

 You can execute **Extract Interface** not only on classes, but on interfaces as well.

Extract Superclass

The **Extract Superclass** refactoring mimics the **Extract Interface** refactoring but, instead of an interface, a superclass will be created. The existing class will be amended to extend the newly created superclass. In the dialog box, select the members you would like to move to the superclass. Again, we have two options here. The first option is that we can just extract the superclass. The second option is to rename the original class, giving the superclass its previous name. IntelliJ IDEA will then scan for its usages and try to use the superclass where possible:

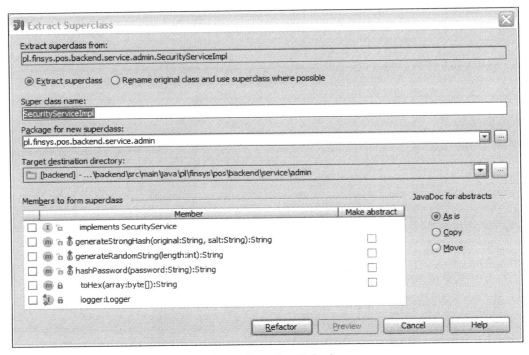

The Extract Superclass dialog box

Inline

The Inline family of refactorings is the exact opposite of the Extract refactorings. The target can be a superclass, local field, or method. Execute the **Inline** refactoring with *Ctrl + Alt + N* (PC) or *cmd + Option + N* (Mac).

If the target you pick is the superclass, IntelliJ IDEA will move all fields from the superclass into its inheritors. The dialog box will show all the inheritors found and give you the option to delete the superclass, as shown in the following screenshot:

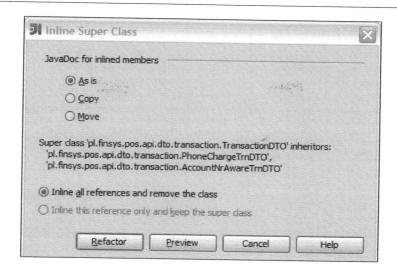

If you pick the field as the target, IntelliJ IDEA will give you the choice to either make all references inline and then remove the field, or to make the only selected reference inline and keep the field, as shown in the following screenshot:

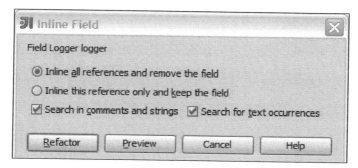

The same dialog box with the **Inline Method** selected is shown in the next screenshot; you will be able to make all invocations inline and then remove the method:

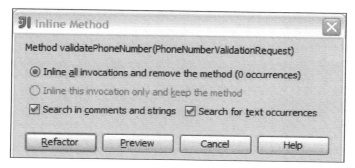

Remove Middleman

This is the opposite of the **Delegate** refactoring. Sometimes, Middleman classes simply take calls and forward them to other components without doing any work. This is an unnecessary layer and can be removed with minimal effort in IntelliJ IDEA. The IDE will analyze the class and, if it detects that a class is being used as a delegate, it will simply replace all calls to the delegating methods with equivalent direct calls. To execute this action, place the cursor on the delegate and then select **Remove Middleman** from the **Refactor** menu. If possible, IntelliJ IDEA will offer to remove the delegating methods if they become obsolete.

Wrap Return Value

The **Wrap Return Value** refactoring will create a wrapper around the method's return value. In the additional options dialog box, you can choose to create a new class or use an existing class, as shown here:

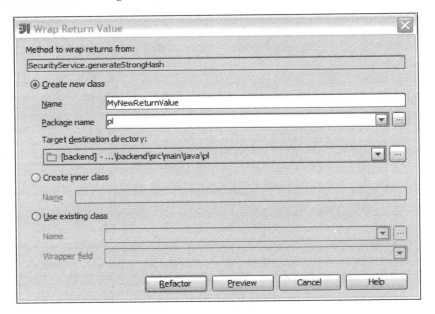

Invert Boolean

The **Invert Boolean** refactoring allows you to quickly invert the logical value of the variable or method that returns a boolean value. It can be quite useful even when you have complicated boolean calculations. Take a look at the following example. Enter the following code before the inversion:

```
private boolean isValid(int a) {
  return a > 15 && a < 100;
}
```

Enter the following code after the inversion:

```
private boolean isValid(int a) {
  return a <= 15 || a >= 100;
}
```

Inverting a boolean value comes in handy when your variables does not reflect what is currently happening or when you want to get cleaner method naming as a preparation for extracting a method.

Pull Members Up or Push Members Down

The **Pull Members Up or Push Members Down** refactorings are especially useful to redesign the class hierarchy. **Pull Members Up** allows you to move members of a class to the superclass or interface. On the other hand, **Push Members Down** will move the class members to a subclass.

In the dialog box, select the members you want to pull up or push down and preview or apply the changes.

Replace Inheritance With Delegation

Replace Inheritance With Delegation is another class hierarchy refactoring. IntelliJ IDEA will create a field that refers to an instance of the superclass. Next, each method defined in the subclass will be amended to use the delegate field.

If your class uses only a part of its superclass, it may be a good candidate to execute **Replace Inheritance With Delegation** on. This way, you promote composition over inheritance, so the behavior of your class is easier to change later.

In the dialog box, set the field name for the delegate and select the methods you want to delegate. Additionally, you may generate accessors for the delegate field, by checking **Generate getter for delegated component**, as shown in the following screenshot:

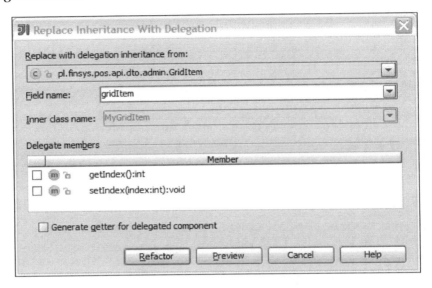

Convert Anonymous Class to Inner

The **Convert Anonymous Class to Inner** refactoring will simply convert an anonymous class to a named inner class. If there are any local variables being accessed in the anonymous class, IntelliJ IDEA will create the constructor for the inner class and pass the local variables using the constructor.

Encapsulate Fields

The **Encapsulate Fields** option will replace direct read and write access to the selected fields with corresponding getter and setter methods. If there are no accessor methods present in the class, they will be generated. Otherwise, the existing methods will be used. In the dialog box, you can choose to encapsulate read or write access and set the encapsulated field's visibility, as shown in the following screenshot:

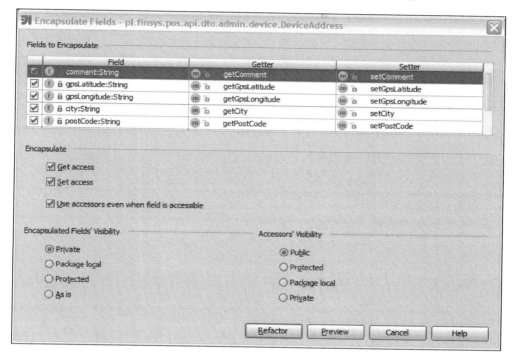

Replace Constructor with Factory Method / Builder

Both these refactorings will form a method that will produce the instance of the class. The constructor calls will then be replaced with calls to this method. The difference is that **Replace Constructor with Factory Method** will create the static factory method and **Replace Constructor with Builder** will produce the instance method in the new class or in some other existing class. In the dialog box, you can enter a new class name or point to the existing class you would like to create the method in, as shown in the following screenshot:

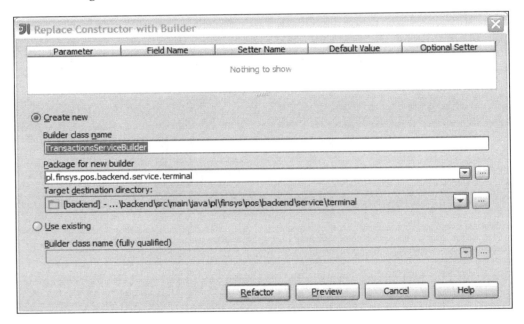

Generify

The **Generify** option will transform source code that does not use Java generics in the code that does. IntelliJ IDEA will analyze the code and, according to the options selected, will introduce generic types into the selected class. In the **Generify** options dialog box, you can customize refactoring action behavior such as dropping obsolete casts and producing wildcard types, as shown in the following screenshot:

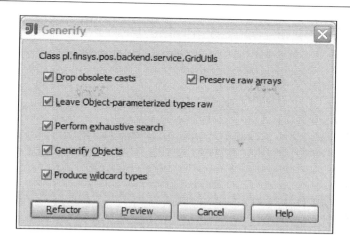

As usual, nothing beats using keyboard shortcuts when it comes to performance, so let's summarize refactoring keyboard shortcuts in the following table:

Action	PC shortcut	Mac shortcut
Copy	*F5*	*F5*
Move	*F6*	*F6*
Safe delete	*Alt + Delete*	*cmd + delete*
Rename	*Shift + F6*	*Shift + F6*
Type Migration	*Ctrl + Shift + F6*	*cmd + Shift + F6*
Change Signature	*Ctrl + F6*	*cmd + F6*
Inline	*Ctrl + Alt + N*	*cmd + option + N*
Extract Method	*Ctrl + Alt + M*	*cmd + option + M*
Introduce Variable	*Ctrl + Alt + V*	*cmd + option + V*
Introduce Field	*Ctrl + Alt + F*	*cmd + option + F*
Introduce Constant	*Ctrl + Alt + C*	*cmd + option + C*
Introduce Parameter	*Ctrl + Alt + P*	*cmd + option + P*

Summary

In this chapter, we covered powerful refactoring functionalities in IntelliJ IDEA. By now, you should have a fairly good idea what refactoring in IntelliJ IDEA is all about. Using the actions from the refactoring toolset will help you make code cleaner, more maintainable, and easy to extend. Thanks to its advanced code analysis, IntelliJ IDEA can perform most refactorings automatically, saving significant time. However, it's not only about the speed but also about the confidence you can have with the IDE altering your source code. Most of the time, automatic refactorings performed in IntelliJ IDEA are smart and safe.

Feel free to experiment by selecting targets and refactoring actions. Remember that you can always undo.

Now you know how to make your code refactored and clean, so the next step will be to run it. We will do this in the next chapter.

5
Make It Happen – Running Your Project

In IntelliJ IDEA, you can run or debug your project in numerous ways. In this chapter, we will focus on creating runtime configurations and explain its options. We will cover topics such as running a standalone application, a web application using the Tomcat server, and to step out of the Java world for a while, the Node.js application. This chapter will give you an overview of the configuration dialog boxes and make it easier for you to create your own configurations.

Each run or debug configuration is the named set of parameters IntelliJ IDEA will use to run your application. The IDE comes with some predefined settings. By installing the corresponding plugin, you can extend the IDE runtime features even further. We covered the installing process of plugins in *Chapter 1, Get to Know Your IDE Fast*.

The run/debug configurations in IntelliJ IDEA are categorized into temporary and permanent. Let's start with the temporary one because this is the type of run configuration that you will probably work with most often.

A temporary configuration

The temporary setup is created by the selected environment when you select **Run** or **Debug** on a particular element, such as a Java class or test class for example. To create a temporary configuration, use the *Ctrl + Shift + F10* (PC) or *control + Shift + R* (Mac) shortcuts, or just right-click on a particular element and select **Run** or **Debug** from the context menu, as shown in the following screenshot:

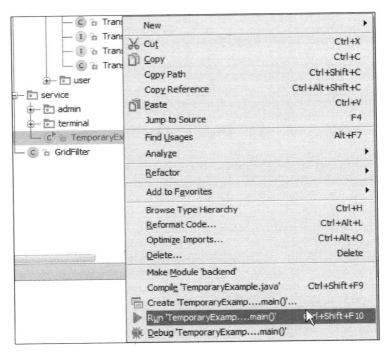

You can also create a temporary configuration by right-clicking on a single test method, a main method in the editor window, or a Maven target in the Maven sidebar window. After executing the temporary profile for the first time, it gets added in the **Run** menu, along with your permanent configurations, as shown in the following screenshot. Take note that the icon of the temporary configuration will be semitransparent to easily distinguish it from the permanent configuration that we will describe in a while.

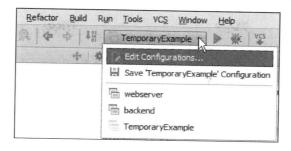

By default, IntelliJ IDEA will store up to five different temporary configurations. They will persist across restarts.

> It is usually much more efficient to start with a temporary run configuration and convert it into a permanent one later. You can get a 90 percent complete configuration by right-clicking somewhere in your code and selecting the **Run...** entry in the context menu. Starting from here will take much less time than starting from scratch.

At any time, the temporary configuration can be converted to a permanent one by using the **Save Configuration** item in the **Run** drop-down menu. Let's talk about the permanent configurations now.

The permanent configuration

To edit configurations, open the **Edit Configurations** screen from the **Run** menu:

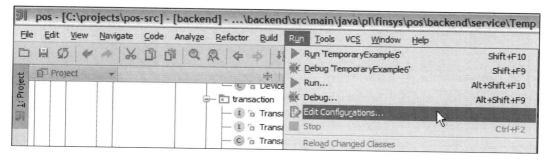

The **Edit Configurations** screen will open. On the left pane, there is the list of created configurations contained within the groups. To create a new configuration setup, click on the green plus icon (**+**) or use the *Alt + Insert* (PC) or *cmd + N* (Mac) keyboard shortcut:

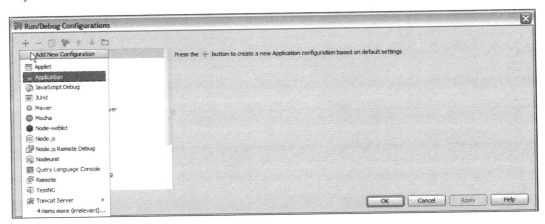

The list of possible configuration types depends on the installed plugins. If you cannot find the specific type, install the corresponding plugin first. To give you an overview of how to create runtime or debug configuration, we will define the standard Java application profile now.

The Run/Debug configuration for a Java application

Select **Application** from the **Add New Configuration** list to see your new **Unnamed** configuration in the **Application** group. On the pane towards the right of the dialog box, the IDE will present the details of the newly created configuration.

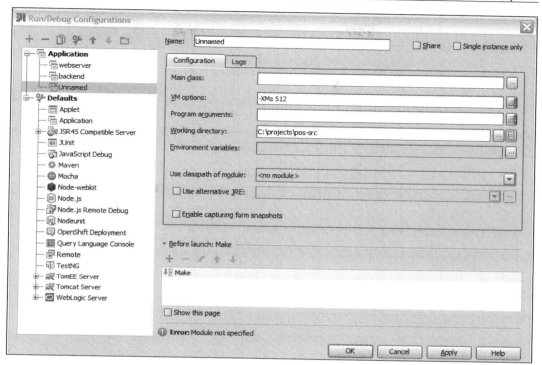

In the **Name** field, you give the configuration a name under which the configuration will be available later in the **Run** drop-down menu:

If you select the **Single instance only** checkbox every time your run your project, IntelliJ IDEA will check whether there is a configuration of that type already running. If so, the IDE will display the confirmation dialog box asking whether you want to stop the currently running instance and execute it again:

This can be useful especially if the runtime configuration uses resources that can be allocated only one at a time, such as the listening ports in the web server.

The **Share** checkbox allows you to share your configuration. We'll talk more about sharing configurations later in this chapter.

In the **Main class** field, you specify the fully qualified name of the class to be executed, which contains the main() method. Using the *Shift + Enter* keyboard shortcut will bring out the **Choose Main Class** dialog box, helping you find a specific class.

> The *Shift + Enter* keyboard shortcut works in all these text fields that have a small button next to them, which pops up an additional window to insert data.

You can search for a class by name or in the project tree. As usual, just start entering the text to narrow the list down:

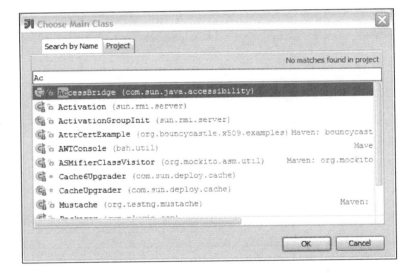

If you need to pass **VM options** to the executing application, use the **VM options** field. Separate multiple options with a space. The button after the **VM options** text field will open up a small dialog box where you can edit **VM options** line by line. This is useful if you have many **VM options** to edit. IntelliJ IDEA will pass those **VM options** to the Java Virtual Machine just before executing the application, for example `-Xmx1024m` or `-Dlogback.configurationFile`, as shown here:

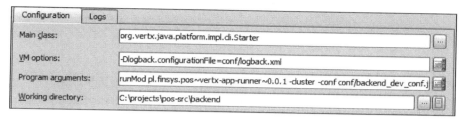

 If the **VM options** text box includes spaces, enclose the argument in double quotes. If the option includes double quotes, escape them with backslashes.

By default, the working directory of the application will be the directory containing the project file. This directory will be the base for all relative input and output file paths. To select another directory, use the **Working directory** field or click on the **Browse** button as shown here:

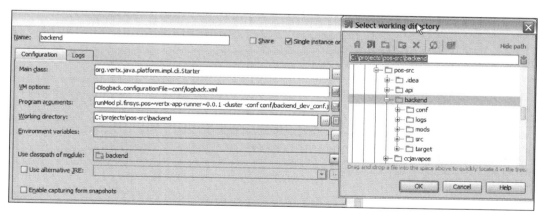

As you already know from *Chapter 2, Off We Go – To the Code*, the project structure consists of the modules. The **Use classpath of module** drop-down list allows you to select the module that the classpath of IntelliJ IDEA will use to execute the application, as shown in the following screenshot:

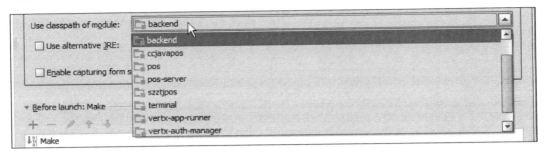

The configuration dialog box allows you to specify an alternative JRE to be used with this specific run/debug configuration. To use this feature, mark the **Use alternative JRE** checkbox and pick the desired runtime environment from the list, as shown in the following screenshot:

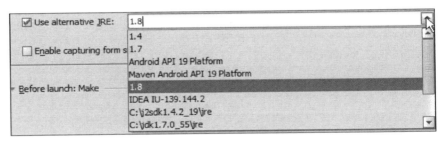

If you want some specific tasks to be executed before running the profile, use the **Before launch** section of the dialog box. By default, the only task before executing the application is the **Make** task. IntelliJ IDEA will automatically make the project before launching. The other options include executing the external tool or Maven task, for example. Any other configuration can be executed before as well. You can add multiple items to the list and reorder them. The possibilities are endless here.

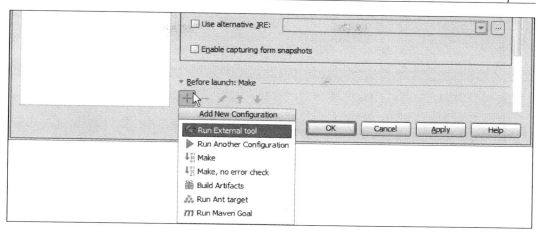

In the **Logs** tab, you can specify which of the log files generated by the running application should be displayed in the console. By default, IntelliJ IDEA will display a standard output on the console, but you can add a specific logfile to be shown in the console as well. To add a log file, just use the *Alt + Insert* keyboard shortcut, create an alias, and select the file to be included in the console output as shown here:

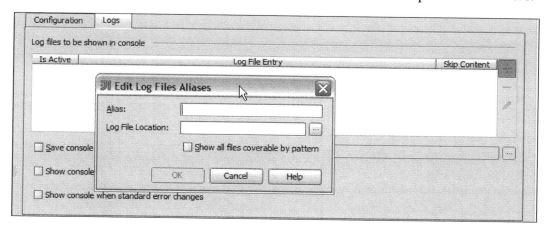

To activate the output console and bring it forward if an associated process writes to Standard.out or Standard.err, select the corresponding checkboxes as shown here:

This was the general Java application setup. To give you an idea of how to configure different types of runtime configurations, let's take a look at how to configure the web application profile using the local Tomcat server as an example.

Creating a Tomcat server local configuration

The Ultimate edition of IntelliJ IDEA is capable of running your projects using different application servers. To create a local Tomcat server configuration, select **Tomcat/Local** from the **Add New Configuration** pane of the **Run/Debug Configurations** dialog box, as shown in the following screenshot:

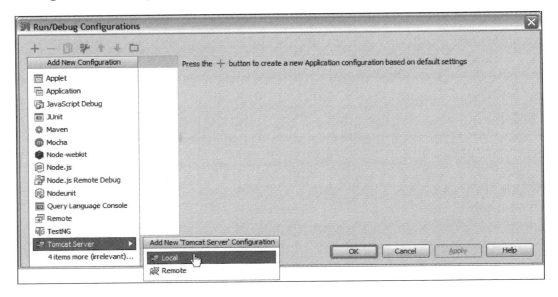

This time, the details pane of the configuration will be specific to the Tomcat server, as shown in the following screenshot:

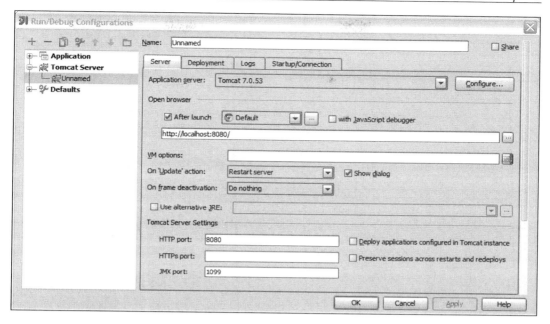

Again, you provide the configuration name. This name will then be present in the **Run** menu.

In the **Server** tab, you can configure **VM options** and the ports Tomcat will be listening on. You can also specify the action that will be taken when updating the web application on the server or the frame deactivation. The frame deactivation switches from IntelliJ IDEA to a different application.

 Choose **Update classes and resources** on the frame deactivation to have the classes and resources of your application reloaded automatically when you switch from IntelliJ IDEA to the web browser.

In the **Application server** drop-down list, there are instances of the configured Tomcat application servers. If needed, the new application server can be added to the list using the **Configure** button. Click on the button and point to your local server installation directory. IntelliJ IDEA will then pick up the required libraries and create the application server instance in the IDE, as shown in the following screenshot:

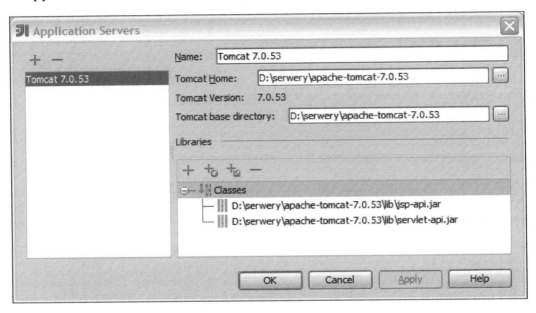

It may be convenient to have the web browser of your choice started with the URL of your application. To do this automatically, check the **After launch** checkbox as shown in the following screenshot:

On the second **Deployment** tab, you can specify what will be deployed on the chosen server during startup. In the Tomcat server, the external source or the artifact can be deployed. We were talking about artifacts in *Chapter 2, Off We Go – To the Code*. To add the item to be deployed, use the *Alt + Insert* shortcut or click on the green plus icon (**+**). You can specify under which context URL each artifact should be deployed in the Tomcat application server, as shown in the following screenshot:

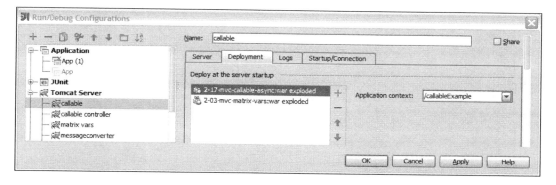

The **Logs** tab is very similar to the tab we saw in the normal Java application profile. This time, however, we have some predefined logfiles present in the list, taken from the chosen Tomcat application server picked in the first tab as shown here:

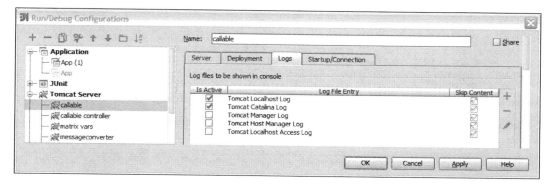

Finally, the last tab, **Startup/Connection**, allows you to tweak the application server startup and shutdown routines. The default scripts presented here are usually very good out of the box, but if you want to change the procedure, just uncheck the **Use default** checkbox and provide your own scripts, as shown in the following screenshot. IntelliJ IDEA will use these scripts to launch and stop the server.

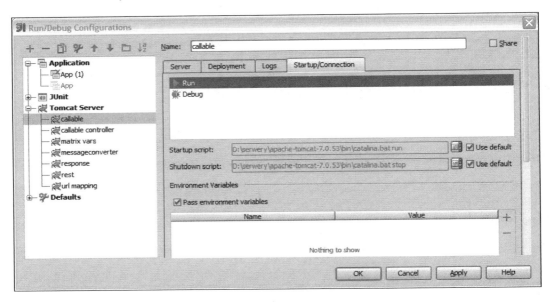

We covered setting up the runtime configuration of the local Tomcat server. From now on, you can easily develop, run, and debug Java web applications. However, IntelliJ IDEA is not only about Java. If you have a corresponding plugin installed, you can create runtime configuration profiles for other technologies and languages as well. Let's take a look at how to create the Node.js runtime setup as an example.

The Node.js configuration

Pick Node.js from the list of available configuration templates:

Node.js is totally different from Java, so the runtime/debug configuration dialog box is totally different as well. Only some of the possible options are common with the other runtime configurations: the configuration name, the **Before launch** section mentioned earlier, and the **Share/Single instance only** option.

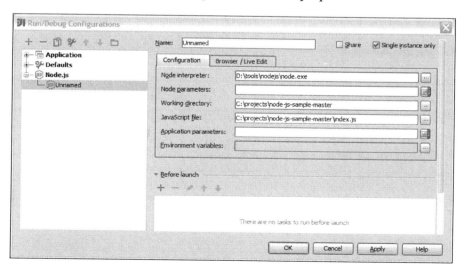

In the corresponding fields, you need to point to the node interpreter installed locally to set up the working directory. In the **JavaScript file** field, you should enter the application's starting point file that you want IntelliJ IDEA to execute. Type the paths manually or use the "browsing" buttons on the right.

If your Node.js application has the web/HTML user interface, you can make IntelliJ IDEA run the web browser of your choice in the second tab, which is **Browser / Live Edit.**

If you end up having many run/debug configurations, you can create folders in the **Run/Debug Configurations** dialog box and organize them.

> You can organize your configurations by moving them into the folders by dragging them using the mouse.

In **Run/Debug Configurations**, one of the groups is the special group. This is the **Defaults** group, which we will discuss now.

Configuration defaults

In the **Defaults** group, you can edit the default configuration options that IntelliJ IDEA will copy later to every specific configuration you create. Actually, changing the default settings is rarely needed, but in case you need to do this, the IDE gives you this possibility. Take note that these changes are applied to newly created configurations only.

> The settings defined in the **Defaults** node of the **Run/Debug Configurations** dialog box will be used in permanent and temporary configurations.

To create the default setup, expand the **Defaults** node, select the desired runtime type and fill out the form towards the right hand side of the on-screen window. For example, if you select the **Default/Application** configuration, you can edit Java VM options or environment variables that IntelliJ IDEA will then duplicate to every new profile, as shown in the following screenshot:

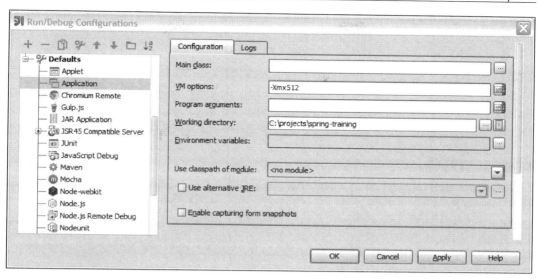

Note that the list of available default configuration types reflects the possible configuration types you can create and depends on the plugins you installed.

Sharing the configuration

If you decide to share your runtime or debug setup and make it available to the other team members, select the **Share** checkbox as shown in the following screenshot:

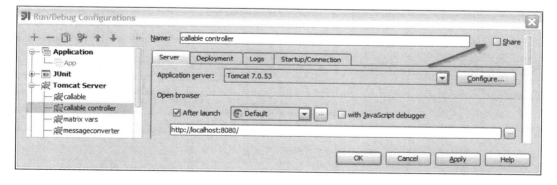

If you mark the **Share** checkbox and the directory-based format is used, IntelliJ IDEA will save the run/debug configuration in a separate file in the `runConfiguration` folder. On the other hand, if you use the file-based format, the runtime/debug configuration will be saved in the `.ipr` file. You can throw the runtime configuration into the version control then.

If you have your run/debug configuration defined, it's time to run the application.

Running

To run the specific run/debug configuration, pick it from the **Run** drop-down menu and choose **Run** from the toolbar or hit the *Shift + F10* (PC) or *control + R* (Mac) keyboard shortcut.

You can also use *Alt + Shift + F10* (PC) or *control + Option + R* (Mac) to see a handy pop up with all the defined configurations for you to pick and then run. Additionally, the first item on the pop up is **Edit Configurations…**, which is a nice shortcut to open the **Run/Debug** configuration dialog box.

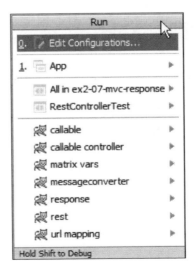

The results of the launch will be presented in the **Run** tool window, which is placed at the bottom of the workspace by default, as shown in the following screenshot:

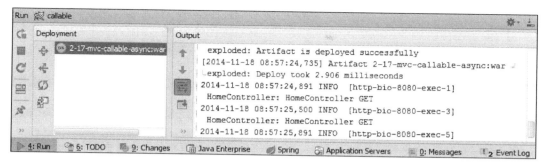

The largest part of the **Run** tool window is occupied by the **Console** view (in case of a standalone Java application) or the **Output** view (in case of a web application). The standard output will presented here. The buttons on the left side of the **Console** or **Output** view allow clearing the view, toggling the line wrapping, or printing the content. If you had specified the additional log files in the configuration dialog box, the log files will be presented in the corresponding tabs.

 Displaying many logs in the console impacts performance—it will slow down the execution of your application.

The buttons towards the left will let you stop, restart, or pause the execution and also pin the **Run** tool window.

 The pinned results of a previous run will not be overwritten by a new run. This is especially helpful when running unit tests as you can run all the tests, pin the test results, and then fix failing tests one by one without losing the information about the tests that still need to be fixed.

On the other hand, the **Debug** tool window is a little bit more complicated; we will cover it in detail in *Chapter 8, Squash'em – The Debugger*.

Summary

In this chapter, you learned how to create runtime or debug configurations for your project. The configuration editor in IntelliJ IDEA is very flexible and allows you to freely tweak runtime parameters, environment variables, and options.

Until now, you used the automatic build process supported by the IDE. In the next chapter, you will learn how to make IntelliJ IDEA use the build files we provide using Maven or Gradle.

6
Building Your Project

You can build and package your project in several ways in IntelliJ IDEA. In this chapter, we will focus on building a project using external tools like Maven and Gradle. Maven is the industry standard to build Java projects nowadays, so we will focus our attention on it and discuss how IntelliJ IDEA makes your work with Maven more simple and intuitive. The Maven build file is a first-class citizen in IntelliJ IDEA. The best thing is that if you use Maven or Gradle to build your application in IntelliJ IDEA, you will be able to build the project outside of the IDE as well. If you are new to Maven, check out their website at http://maven.apache.org, and for Gradle, take a look at http://www.gradle.org.

We will cover the following topics in this chapter:

- Editing Maven settings
- The **Maven** tool window
- Executing Maven goals and plugins
- Editing Gradle settings
- Executing Gradle tasks

We already mentioned how to import the Maven project and manage its dependencies in *Chapter 2, Off We Go – To the Code*. Let's take a closer look at how to edit Maven settings and how to actually execute the build or single tasks.

Editing Maven settings

The Maven project settings can be configured at two levels: for the current project and the project template. For the current project, select **Settings** from **File** (PC) or navigate to **IDEA | Preferences** (Mac). The settings dialog box will pop up, where you need to navigate to **Build, Execution, Deployment | Build Tools | Maven**, as shown in the following screenshot:

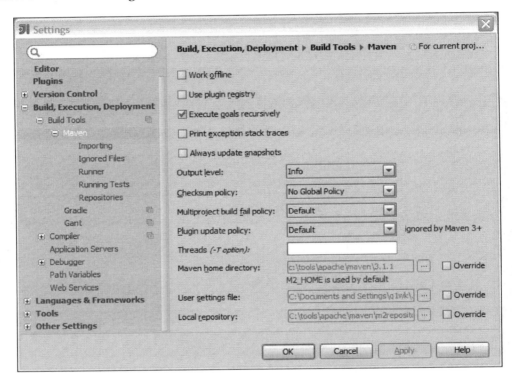

 You can also start typing Maven in the search box in the **Settings** dialog box to quickly go to the **Maven** settings page.

If you want to define settings for the default project template, choose **Maven** by navigating to **File | Other Settings | Default Settings**. These settings will be used as the default settings every time a Maven project is imported or a new Maven module is created. Most of the settings are the equivalents for the Maven command-line switches.

Let's now examine the Maven settings in detail. On each launch, Maven looks into the remote repositories and checks for updates. Executing a Maven goal can result in downloading new archives. To avoid this behavior, check **Work offline**. Maven will then use resources that are only available locally. If something is missing, it will report the problems. The **Work offline** checkbox is the equivalent of the --offline Maven switch command line.

 The offline mode is useful when you need to work offline or when your network connection is slow.

IntelliJ IDEA determines the Maven home directory from the M2_HOME environment variable. This can be overridden by selecting the **Override** checkbox and entering a fully qualified name for the Maven installation directory. You can also browse for the location using the ellipsis browse button. The Maven settings IntelliJ IDEA will use are taken from the settings.xml file in the .m2 folder of your home directory. If you need to specify other settings for the project, check the **Override** checkbox again and provide another location for the settings.xml file.

The local Maven repository refers to a copy on your own installation, which is a cache of the remote downloads and temporary build artifacts that are not yet released. By default, it resides in the Repository folder in the .m2 folder of your home directory. To override the location, mark the **Override** checkbox and provide the other location.

To set the policy to deal with checksum matching while downloading the artifacts, use the **Checksum Policy** option. The **Fail** value, which is equivalent to the --strict-checksums command-line option, will fail the download if the checksums do not match. If you just want a warning to be printed, set it to the **Warn** value (equal to --lax-checksums).

Two options can be useful if you have a multiproject build file. The first one, **Execute goals recursively**, enabled by default, makes the build recur into the nested projects. On the contrary, if you uncheck this option, Maven will behave like it behaves with the --non-recursive command-line switch.

The second option, **Multiproject build fail policy**, specifies how Maven should behave in the case of a build failure: at the very first failure (the`--fail-fast` command-line option) or **Fail at the end** (the`--fail-at-end` command-line option). The last value, **Ignore failures** (the`--fail-never` command-line option), will make the build process never fail, regardless of the result.

If you want the output of the build process to be more verbose, two options can come in handy (they are basically the -x switch of Maven):

- **Print exception stack traces** will make Maven generate the complete stack trace in the case of a failure.

- **Output level** will set the Maven logger to the desired level, with the Debug value being the most verbose.

Sometimes a specific version of the plugins is needed to build your project. In such cases, you can make Maven use the plugin registry. The plugin registry configuration is located usually in `plugin-registry.xml` in the `.m2` folder. This configuration is disabled by default. To enable it, check the **Use plugin registry** checkbox. Refer to the Maven documentation to get details about the plugin registry.

> To make IntelliJ IDEA always update fresh snapshots from the remote repository, check the **Always update snapshots** checkbox. This is inadvisable when you are using a project with many snapshot dependencies. Downloading new snapshots on every build will take a lot of time.

If your project is huge and you would like to speed up the build process, you may try using a parallelized build. To do this, provide a value in the **Threads (-T option)** field. This is equivalent to the -T Maven option. The performance boost depends deeply on your module structure, but according to the Maven documentation, 20 to 50 percent speed improvement is quite common. Use the number as a parameter to provide the number of threads to be run or use the C option to provide the number of threads per core. For example, -T 4 will execute the build with four threads and using -T 1C will execute the build with one thread per CPU core.

> If your build runs slowly, consider executing it with more threads.

On the **Ignored Files** page, you can specify the file types and individual files that will not be included in the build process.

The **Import** page is identical to the one displayed when you import your project from the Maven model. If you mark **Keep projects files in** and specify the directory, IntelliJ IDEA will create .iml and .idea in the specified directory. This option is not selected by default; IntelliJ IDEA will create its project files next to the pom.xml files. If **Create module groups for multi-module Maven projects** is selected, IntelliJ IDEA will create a module group from the parent Maven project with the nested modules included in the group. As you may remember, the **Import Maven projects automatically** option will force IntelliJ IDEA to automatically synchronize its own project structure each time your pom.xml is modified.

The **Runner** page gives you the possibility to tweak the external Maven configuration that will be used to run goals. For example, you can pick the JRE that will be used to execute the build goal. You can also specify Java VM options that will be passed to this JRE.

 As usual, if the VM option contains spaces, wrap the spaces or the argument that contains them with double quotes. If an option includes double quotes, avoid the double quotes with backslashes.

The **Skip tests** option is the equivalent of the Maven -Dmaven.test.skip=true command-line switch and will result, as the name suggests, in no test being executed during the build.

The last page of the **Maven** settings dialog box is the list of local and remote repositories. The table shows the list of repositories discovered in the loaded project. Here, you can find the URLs of the local and remote repositories, type (local or remote), and the date of the latest update.

Now that we have explained our Maven options, let's take a look at the **Maven** tool window.

The Maven tool window

If you work with Maven projects, the Maven tool window will probably be one of your most used windows. You can use it to run Maven goals, execute plugins, and browse the dependencies. Execute the Maven tool window by navigating to **View | Tool Windows** as shown here:

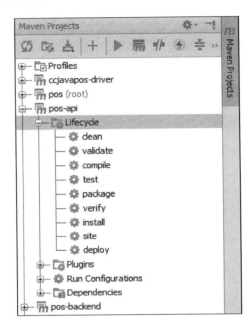

We will now use this tool window to execute Maven goals and plugins.

Running Maven goals

In IntelliJ IDEA, you can run specific Maven goals in two ways: either by creating the run/debug configuration or running it directly from the **Maven** tool window. To run the selected goal, expand the **Lifecycle** branch in the **Maven** tool window and choose **Run Maven Build** from the context menu, as shown in the following screenshot:

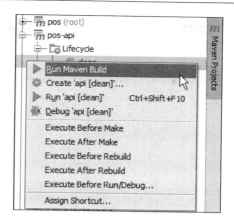

If you choose **Create** from the context menu, the permanent run configuration to run this goal will be produced. The **Create Run/Debug** configuration will show up, allowing you to tweak the parameters of the newly created run configuration.

 Basically, you need to create a permanent run configuration for a Maven goal if you try to run that goal with non-standard options (for example, if you need to add certain parameters).

On the other hand, picking **Run** or **Debug** will execute the build and then create a temporary configuration you can save later as a permanent one. We described temporary and permanent configurations in detail in the previous chapter. Refer to this chapter for directions on how to deal with the **Run/Debug** configurations.

You can also run a specific goal by selecting it and pressing the *Ctrl + Shift + F10* (PC) or *control + Shift + R* (Mac) keyboard shortcut.

 You can assign your own keyboard shortcut to run a specific goal.

To create a shortcut, select **Assign shortcut...** from the menu. In the **Keymap** dialog box, the selected goal will be highlighted; pick the desired shortcut type from the context menu, as shown in the following screenshot:

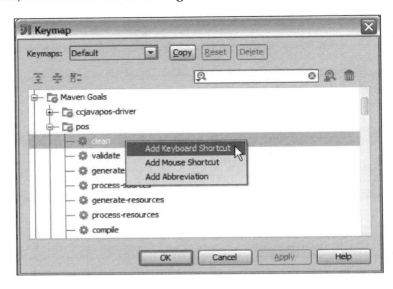

As well as running goals, you can also execute Maven plugins defined in the pom. xml file. Just expand the **Plugins** branch of the module tree, select the desired plugin, and then pick the action from the context menu. The same rules as the running goals apply here; **Run Maven Build** will just execute the plugin, **Create** will create the permanent configuration, and **Run** or **Debug** will create the temporary run or debug configuration:

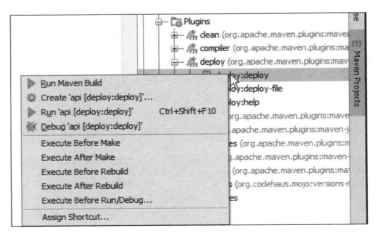

The result of the goal or plugin execution will be presented in the **Run** tool window, as shown here:

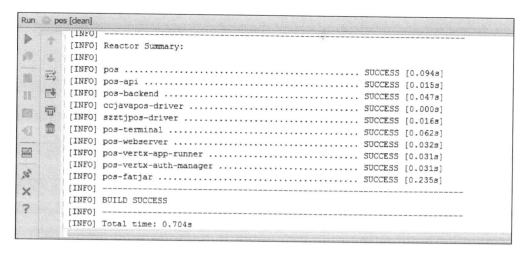

The goal execution window is the typical **Run** tool window we described in the previous chapter. It will present the whole build process output with the build summary at the end. Basically, this is the exact output you would get if you execute Maven from outside IntelliJ IDEA in the OS shell.

 You can also use the embedded terminal in IntelliJ IDEA to execute Maven goals. Make sure you have the terminal plugin enabled.

The **Maven** tool window can also be used to download documentation and source codes for the dependencies defined in the pom.xml file. To download sources or documentation, select the toolbar icon in the **Maven** tool window, as shown in the following screenshot:

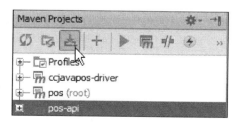

To download sources or documentation for individual dependencies, expand the **Dependencies** branch and pick the desired action from the context menu as shown here:

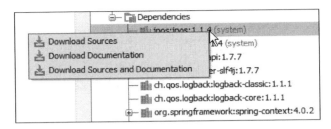

Downloaded sources and documentation will then be used by IntelliJ IDEA to provide completion and Javadoc hints in the editor.

Now that we have covered Maven in IntelliJ IDEA, let's take a look at the alternative build tool, Gradle. Gradle, powered by the Groovy language, is quickly becoming the build system of choice for many open source and commercial projects. IntelliJ IDEA supports Gradle in a similar way it supports Maven.

Using Gradle

To use Gradle, you must first enable the **Gradle** and **Groovy** plugins in the IDE settings. Refer to *Chapter 1, Get to Know Your IDE, Fast*, for information on how to enable the required plugins.

The second thing you need to do is link your project to the Gradle project. If an IntelliJ IDEA project is not linked to a Gradle project, then the **Gradle** tool window will be disabled and IntelliJ IDEA will display the prompt:

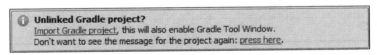

Select **Import Gradle project**, point to `build.gradle`, and you are all set. The Gradle tool window will become available. Later, if you decide to change the Gradle settings for the project, you can do so by picking **Settings** from the **File** (PC) menu or by navigating to **IDEA | Preferences** (Mac) and then to **Build, Execution, Deployment | Build Tools | Gradle**. The **Gradle** configuration settings window will show up as follows:

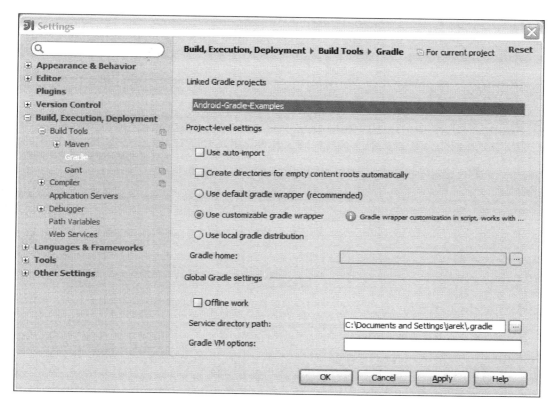

 Start typing `Gradle` in the search box in the **Settings** dialog box to quickly go to the **Gradle** settings page.

In the **Gradle** window, you specify the Gradle project settings. Select the **Use auto-import** checkbox to make IntelliJ IDEA determine all the changes made to the Gradle project automatically every time you refresh your project.

In the Gradle world, the Gradle wrapper is the preferred way to start a Gradle build. The wrapper is a batch script on Windows, and a shell script for other operating systems. Checking the value of **Use gradle wrapper (recommended)** will make IntelliJ IDEA start a Gradle build via the wrapper. Gradle will then be automatically downloaded and used to run the build. On the other hand, **Use customizable gradle wrapper** will allow you to use the custom Gradle wrapper.

Similar to Maven, the **Offline work** switch will make Gradle work offline. The needed dependencies will be taken from the cache, and if any required dependency is not present in the cache, the build will fail.

IntelliJ IDEA determines the Gradle installation path from the GRADLE_HOME or PATH environment variables. If you would like to override the location, click on the browse button in the **Gradle home** field and point to the location or specify the fully qualified path to your Gradle installation manually.

Use the **Gradle VM options** field to pass additional options to the JRE running Gradle. Again, wrap spaces in double quotes and avoid double quotes with backslashes.

Executing Gradle tasks

In the **Gradle** tool window, double-click on your linked Gradle project to expand the branch with the Gradle tasks available. Double-clicking on the task will execute it. You can also click on the task using the right-mouse button and select **Run** or **Debug** from the context menu or use the *Ctrl + Shift + F10* (PC) or *control + Shift + R* (Mac) keyboard shortcut; the screen will look as shown here:

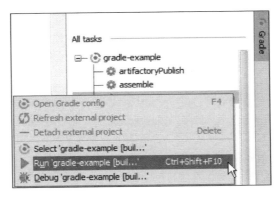

As with Maven goals, a specific Gradle task can be used to create a permanent run/debug configuration. Just pick **Create…** from the context menu to open the **Create Run/Debug Configuration** dialog box.

If you run or debug the Gradle task, it will be listed on the **Recent tasks** list for your convenience at the top of the **Gradle** tool window:

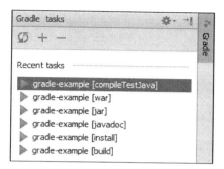

You can run a task by selecting it and using the *Ctrl + Shift + F10* (PC) or *control + Shift + R* (Mac) keyboard shortcut or by double-clicking on it.

The output of executing the task—as with the Maven output—will be presented in the typical **Run** tool window.

Summary

In this chapter, you learned how to use Maven and Gradle to build your project. You can now execute the build process or pick a single goal or plugin to be executed. Maven and Gradle are the most powerful build tools, and having them integrated in the IDE makes using them a lot more convenient.

The next chapter will cover testing. IntelliJ IDEA is designed to support developers and teams who incorporate unit testing in their software development practices. We will create and execute unit tests using JUnit and TestNG.

7
Red or Green? Test Your Code

Usually, we run our unit tests from the build script. However, having the possibility to run them from the IDE can come in handy—one can jump to the failing class and start fixing bugs in no time. In IntelliJ IDEA, you can test your applications using multiple test frameworks. In this chapter, we will focus on installing plugins to test libraries, create tests, and set the runtime configuration to run them. After reading this chapter, you will be able to execute unit tests and include them in your workflow. Let's start with activating the needed plugins.

Enabling the testing plugins

Before you start, make sure you have the needed plugins installed and activated. Plugins for the most common testing libraries, such as JUnit, TestNG, and Karma are bundled in IntelliJ IDEA. Make sure that you have them activated in the **Plugins** dialog box in **Settings**:

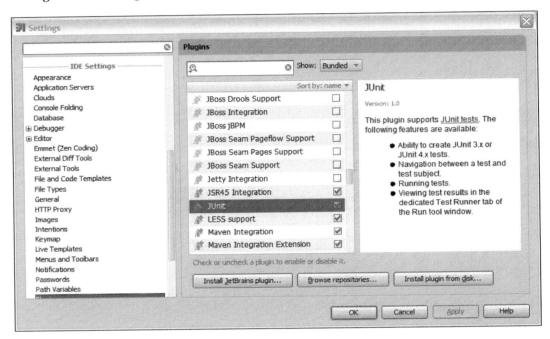

If you skipped the installation of these plugins when you set up the IDE, click on **Install Jetbrains plugin**, select **Unit Testing** from the **Category** drop-down menu, and install them as shown in the following screenshot:

There are many other plugins used for unit testing coming from third-party authors. Click on **Browse repositories**, select **Unit Testing** from the **Category** drop-down menu, and install the desired plugin, as shown in the following screenshot. There is a big chance you will find the plugin to test a library of your choice—even the exotic one.

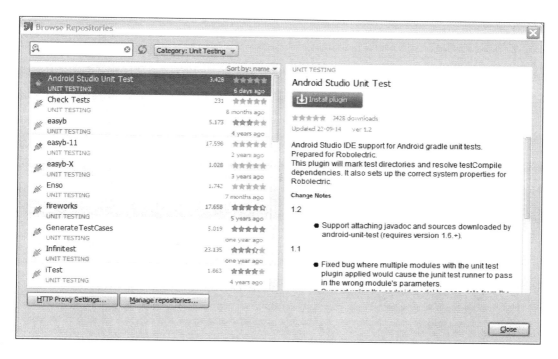

If you install a plugin for a specific framework, IntelliJ IDEA will provide support for it. This will include code completion, the ability to create run/debug configurations to run tests (all tests in a directory, specified test classes, or individual test methods).

 Please refer to the first chapter for a general guide on how to manage your installed plugins.

Creating the test

To create the unit test for your class, choose **Test** from the **Navigate** menu.
Alternatively, you can use the *Ctrl + Shift + T* (PC) or *cmd + Shift + T* (Mac) keyboard
shortcut. If the class you have open in the editor doesn't have any unit tests, the
Create New Test dialog box will pop up asking you to create one as shown here:

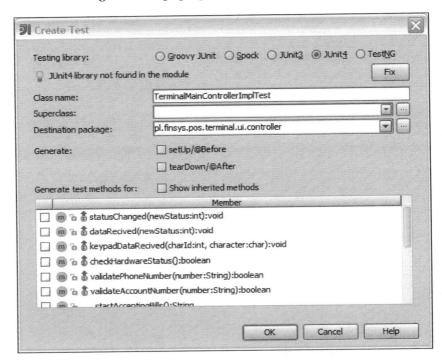

Depending on the plugins installed, the **Testing library** list will differ. Select the
desired library from the list. The libraries for JUnit and TestNG are shipped with
IntelliJ IDEA. Unless you have the testing dependencies defined in your Maven build
file, these libraries will not be included in the classpath of your project or module by
default. IntelliJ IDEA will warn you about this—you can fix this by clicking on the
Fix button. The needed library will then be included to the module classpath. If you
skip this step, the references to the testing library classes and annotations will not be
resolved. In this case, you can do it later in the editor, which we will cover later.

In **Class name**, provide the class name for the unit test. IntelliJ IDEA will add the
`Test` suffix by default. The destination package will be set to the same as the package
of the class to be tested. In Java, this will allow you to have packaged and protected
level access to variables, methods, and constructors of the tested class.

> Depending on the style of tests that you are creating, accessing package
> and protected level variables, methods, and constructors may or may
> not be a good idea. You should be careful not to tie your unit tests too
> much to the implementation details of the class as this will make your
> tests very brittle.

The dialog box will list all the public and protected methods in the class. Select the
ones you want to write tests for.

You can mark the **Generate** checkboxes to set up and tear down methods that have
been generated. If you click on **OK**, a new class will be created with empty methods,
ready for you to fill the test method bodies, as shown in the following screenshot:

```
package pl.finsys.pos.terminal.ui.controller;

import static org.junit.Assert.*;

public class TerminalMainControllerImplTest {

    @org.junit.Before
    public void setUp() throws Exception {

    }

    @org.junit.After
    public void tearDown() throws Exception {

    }

    @org.junit.Test
    public void testStatusChanged() throws Exception {

    }

    @org.junit.Test
    public void testCheckHardwareStatus() throws Exception {

    }
}
```

> Usually, you will have more than one method in your test class testing a
> single method of your class under `test`. Trying to fit everything into a
> single method will make your tests hard to maintain and understand.

If you use the *Alt + Insert* keyboard shortcut inside the test class, you'll be presented with quite an extensive list of typical methods found in test classes that can be autogenerated for you by IntelliJ IDEA, as shown in the following screenshot:

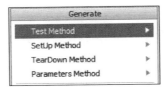

IntelliJ IDEA supports the reverse scenario (the TDD-like one). You can first create a test class and then use IntelliJ IDEA intentions (such as create class, create method, and others) on non-existing (highlighted in red) pieces of test code that you wrote to create these objects (production classes and methods).

 If your monitor has a high enough resolution, another really useful technique when writing tests in a TDD manner is splitting the screen into two halves (**Split Vertically**) and having your test code in the left window and your production code in the right one. Also, in this case, defining additional shortcuts to split and jump between the previous and next splits is very useful.

You switch back to the class being tested by using the *Ctrl + Shift + T* (PC) or *cmd + Shift + T* (Mac) keyboard shortcut. This will give you an option to create another test for the class or navigate to the test you just created, as shown here:

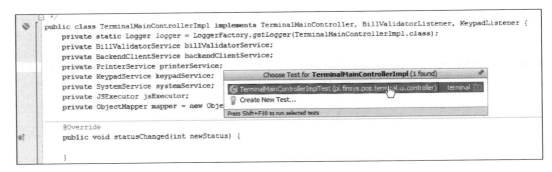

 Using *Ctrl + Shift + T* (PC) or *cmd + Shift + T* (Mac) is a very convenient way to navigate between the class and its unit tests.

If you decided not to include the testing library using the **Create Test** dialog box, you can do it now in the editor. Place the cursor on the unrecognized reference and press *Alt + Enter*. The intention drop-down menu will pop up where you can select **Add library** from the list. IDEA will automatically add the necessary library to the classpath, as shown in the following screenshot:

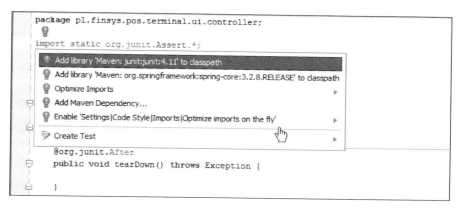

Another way to create a unit test for the class is by using the **Create Test** intention action. This intention action is available in the editor when the cursor is within the line containing the declaration of a class. Navigate to the class you want to test in the editor, place the cursor within the line containing the class declaration, and press *Alt + Enter* to show the list of the intention actions as follows:

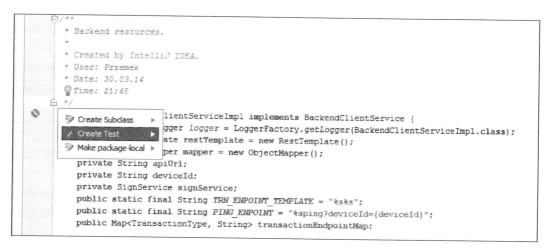

Now choose **Create Test** from the suggestion list to see the same **Create Test** dialog box we described earlier.

> When writing tests, it is really useful to have templates for very common things such as assertions and setting up the mock objects. IntelliJ IDEA comes with a really brilliant templating feature that allows you to make IntelliJ IDEA really smart and context-sensitive; for example, for assertions that are based on the context propose objects. Refer to *Chapter 3, The Editor*, for directions on how to create templates.

Creating a run/debug configuration for the test

In general, IntelliJ IDEA runs and debugs tests in the same way as every other application. The run/debug configuration setup is almost identical to the one we described in *Chapter 5, Make It Happen – Running Your Project*. When the run/debug configuration is created, IntelliJ IDEA passes the individual test classes or methods to the test runner.

The run/debug configuration can be shaped in a number of ways. The first method is to pick the **Edit Configurations...** option from the run configuration's drop-down menu, as shown in the following screenshot:

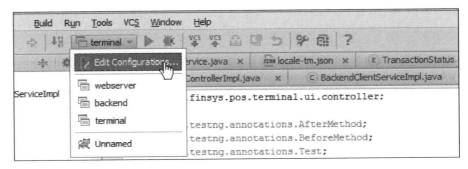

Now you can either click on the green plus icon or use the *Alt + Insert* (PC) or *cmd + N* (Mac) keyboard shortcut. From the list of available run/debug configuration templates, choose the desired test runner configuration as shown here:

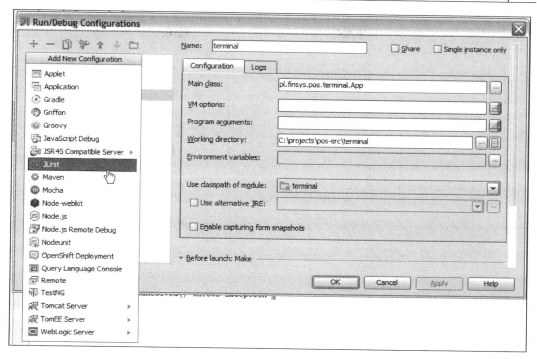

A new unnamed configuration will be created (shown in the following screenshot) allowing you to specify more detailed settings:

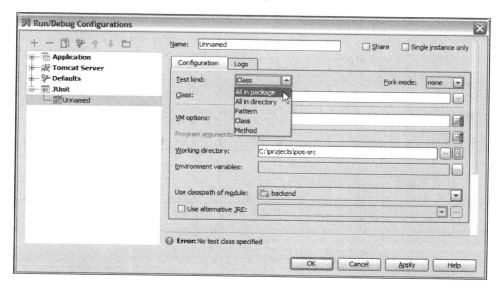

The options will differ according to the testing framework selected, but most of them have the same meaning. In **Test kind**, you can specify what exactly you want to run using this configuration. It can be just a single method in the test class, all tests in the class, all tests in the package, or all tests in the directory. If you choose **All in package** and then the **In whole project** option, IntelliJ IDEA will run tests in all modules of the current project and also include the test you will create in the future.

 Choosing **All in package** or **All in directory** allows you to run multiple test classes under a single run/debug configuration and thus, declutters your run/debug list.

The other options in this dialog box have the same meaning as when you configure a normal application. **VM Options** will make IntelliJ IDEA pass a specified string to the VM to launch the tests. Take note that the `-classpath` option specified in this field overrides the classpath of the module.

The **Working directory** text box specifies the current directory to be used when running a test. This directory defines the starting point for all relative input and output paths.

When needed, the additional environment variables can be passed to the Java virtual machine during the test execution. Place them in the **Environment** variables field.

You can also specify an alternative JRE to run the tests. You usually want your tests to be run in the same Java environment where the classes are being tested. This option, however, allows you to run the same compiled codebase against multiple versions of JRE, which is really useful for applications that support multiple Java versions.

Defining the test run configuration by hand is not very convenient. As you may remember from *Chapter 5, Make It Happen – Running Your Project*, the easier way to create a run configuration is to begin with a temporary one. You can create a test runtime configuration by right-clicking on the test class in the **Project** tool window and picking the **Run** or **Debug** item from the context menu, as shown in the following screenshot:

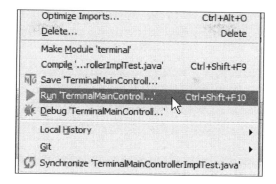

Running the test this way will create a temporary runtime configuration. The temporary configuration will have a semitransparent icon in the configurations list. To save a temporary configuration, choose **Save** from the context menu or the runtime configurations drop-down menu, as shown in the following screenshot:

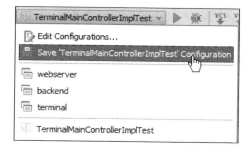

It is also possible to create a run/debug configuration just for a single method in the test class. To do this, open the test class in the editor, place the cursor inside the body of the method you want to create the configuration for, right-click, and then pick **Create** from the context menu as shown here:

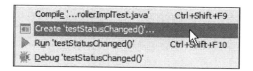

This will also create a temporary runtime configuration; this time for a single test method only.

If you want to create the configuration for multiple tests, the same can be achieved by right-clicking on the same directory in the **Project** tool window and selecting **Run all tests**.

 You can also use the *Ctrl + Shift + F10* (PC) or *control + Shift + R* (Mac) shortcut. It's much quicker — the same shortcut can be used on every level (project, source root, package, class, and method). It makes life much easier when you don't have to use the mouse and you don't have to manually create configurations every time.

Now that we have the test runtime configuration defined, let's execute some tests. The test results will be presented in the tool window we have seen before: the **Run** tool window with the tests results tab.

Running or debugging the test

To start running the test, pick the run configuration you created from the drop-down menu as shown here:

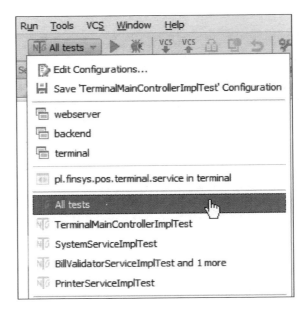

Next, click on the Run icon, select **Run** from the **Run** menu, or just use the *Shift + F10* (PC) or *control + R* (Mac) keyboard shortcut, as you would do with an ordinary application.

> To see the list of available configurations and swiftly select the one you want, use the following keyboard shortcuts: *Shift + Alt + F10* (PC) or *control + option + R* (Mac) for the run configurations, or *Shift + Alt + F9* (PC) or *control + option + D* (Mac) for the debug configurations.

During the execution, the progress bar will show the percentage of tests executed so far.

The test runner status bar indicates whether the tests have passed successfully. It will be green if everything passes and will turn red if at least one of the tests fails.

Sometimes there's a need to debug the test execution. You can debug the test in the same way as you do with every other debug configuration; select it from the configurations drop-down menu and choose **Debug**. Alternatively, just use the *Shift + F9* (PC) or *control + D* (Mac) keyboard shortcut. If the debugger stops on the breakpoint, you will be presented with the **Debugger** tool window, as shown in the following screenshot:

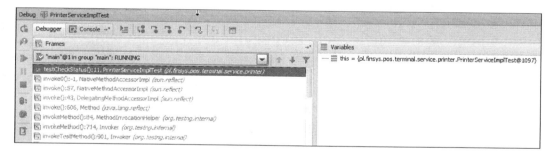

We will cover debugging in detail in *Chapter 8, Squash'em – The Debugger*.

After execution, the tests results will be presented in the **Run** tool window we know from *Chapter 5, Make It Happen – Running Your Project*. This time, the tool window will be a little different; it will contain options and views specific to testing. On the left pane, you can see the list of tests executed; you can expand the list to see a particular test's methods. You can navigate the tests in this pane by using the up arrow and down arrow keys on the keyboard.

To quickly navigate between failing tests only, use the *Ctrl + Alt +* the up arrow key (PC) or *cmd + option +* the up arrow key (Mac), and *Ctrl + Alt +* the down arrow key (PC) or *cmd + option +* the down arrow key (Mac) keyboard shortcuts.

In the right pane of the tool window, there is a console with the test output as shown in the following screenshot:

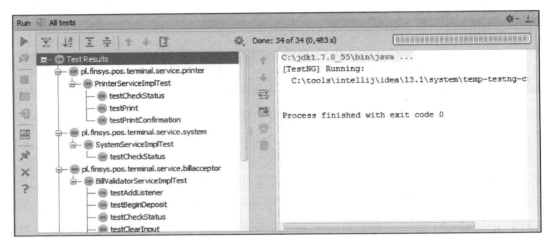

After executing the tests, the message on the IntelliJ IDEA's status bar informs you about the number of failed tests and elapsed time as shown here:

The test runner tab contains the menu with some useful options; open it using the blue cog icon in the toolbar, as shown here:

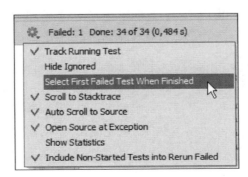

It's good to have **Select First Failed Test When Finished** and **Open Source at Exception** checked to quickly focus on the source code of the failing test in the editor.

Show statistic will open the statistics window, showing the information about the approximate time it took to run the test, as shown here:

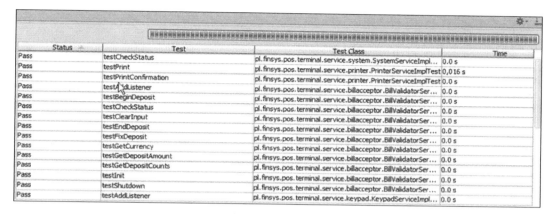

 The **Show statistic** tool window is very helpful to determine slow tests so you can make them faster. Unit tests should run as fast as possible, so you can run them every time you make a change in your project without having to wait a few minutes for the tests to complete.

In the case of test failure, the failing test will be shown with the exclamation icon. IntelliJ IDEA differentiates the failure because of an assertion from the failure due to an error/exception. The assertion failure will show up as an orange exclamation mark and the exception failure will show up as a red one, as shown in the following screenshot:

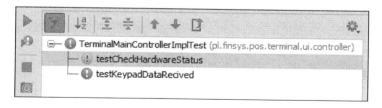

In the console, you will be given the stacktrace of the failing test; this can be seen in the following screenshot:

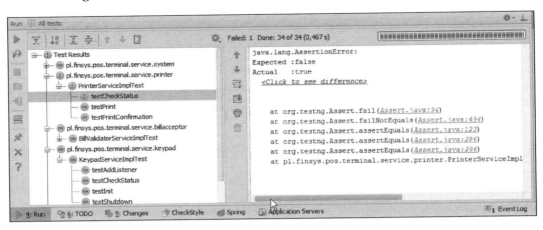

If the test fails because of the assertion error, you will be given the expected and actual value of the assertion in the console pane. The link in the console pane will open the **Comparison Failure** window allowing you to examine the differences in detail. You can also view the difference between the actual and expected value by selecting the failing test and using the *Ctrl + D* keyboard shortcut (the usual shortcut to compare in IntelliJ IDEA) or selecting **View difference** from the context menu, as shown in the following screenshot:

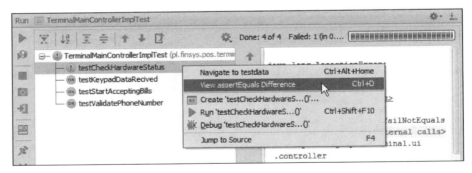

Viewing the difference can be helpful if you have a test framework such as JUnit, where all you can see are assertions. When using more modern test frameworks (such as Spock, for example), you will rarely need to use this feature; if requested, the test framework will provide you with a much better error message.

If you have many tests in a single configuration, it's usually a good idea to hide passing tests to focus better on the failing ones. Select **Hide Passed** to display the failing tests as shown here:

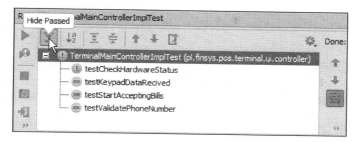

The **Run** and **Debug** tool windows allow rerunning, terminating, and suspending the execution of the tests in the same way as every other application. You can repeat the execution process without leaving the test runner tab of the **Run** tool window. The tests will be executed again using the same run configuration as the initial run. To rerun a testing session, click on the Rerun button on the toolbar of the **Run** tool window or just use the *Ctrl + F5* (PC) or *control + R* (Mac) keyboard shortcut. To rerun only the failed tests, click on **Rerun Failed Tests** as shown here:

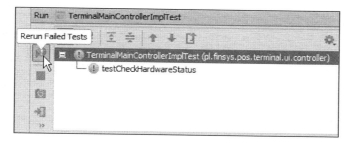

 You can pin the tool window of a previous test run and have the possibility to fix one test after the other. After you have worked on each test, you can run it again and verify that it has been fixed. Without the pin feature, you previous test results will be lost once you run a new test.

As with every other activity in IntelliJ IDEA, remembering some shortcuts comes in handy. Testing is no different—let's summarize the most useful ones now.

Keyboard shortcuts

The following table includes the keyboard shortcuts that covered in this chapter:

Action	PC shortcut	Mac shortcut
Create or navigate to the test	Ctrl + Shift + T	cmd + Shift + T
Select a configuration and run	Alt + Shift + F10	control + option + R
Select a configuration and debug	Alt + Shift + F9	control + option + D
Navigate tests in the Run tool window	The up arrow key / the down arrow key	The up arrow key / The down arrow key
Navigate failed tests in the Run tool window	Ctrl + Alt + the up arrow key / Ctrl + Alt + the down arrow key	cmd + option + the up arrow key / cmd + option + the down arrow key
View assert failure differences	Alt + Enter	Alt + Enter
Run test	Shift + F10	control + R
Debug test	Shift + F9	control + D

Summary

In this chapter, you learned how to set up the testing environment in IntelliJ IDEA. You now know how to import the needed testing library and add it to your project. You can create the test run/debug configuration and navigate in the tests results tool window. In the next chapter, we will focus on the debugger itself, so you can dive into the execution process of your code to quickly find where the potential problem is.

8
Squash'em – The Debugger

Debugging is the process of finding and reducing the number of bugs in your application. In the past, it was a fairly complicated process, sometimes requiring external tools. Today, most programming environments have an integrated debugger, an easy and enjoyable way to find errors in your code. In this chapter, we will focus on the integrated debugger. Out of the box, IntelliJ IDEA supports debugging for Java, Groovy, and JavaScript applications. The debugging functionality is incorporated in IntelliJ IDEA; you only need to configure its settings. Depending on the enabled plugins, the IDE can also support debugging for other languages, for example, Scala or PHP. We will begin by reviewing the debugger settings and options. Setting up the Java and JavaScript debugger will give you a general idea of how to set up the debugger for the language of your choice. Next, we will look at the debugger tool window and then go to the debugging process itself. At the end of the chapter, we will summarize some essential keyboard shortcuts that are valuable for debugging.

After reading this chapter, you will know how to use breakpoints, watches, and how to evaluate expressions. Let's start with the debugger settings.

Debugger settings

At the beginning, you will have to configure the roots, dependencies, and libraries to be passed to the compiler before the debugging process starts. This can be done in the **Project Structure** dialog box. We described the project structure in *Chapter 2, Off We Go – To the Code*. Refer to this chapter to recall how to set up the project structure.

The debugger-related configuration can be found in the **Settings** dialog box, in **Build, Execution, Deployment**. Launch the **Settings** dialog box by picking **Settings** from the **File** menu or just use the *Ctrl + Alt + S* (PC) or *cmd + ,* (Mac) keyboard shortcut.

The important option from the debugging perspective is to make IDEA generate debugging info for the compiled classes. This option is enabled by default; you can find it by navigating to **Java Compiler** | **Generate Debugging Info**.

The debugger itself can be configured in the **Debugger** section. As you may remember, you can quickly find a specific option by entering search keywords in the search field of the **Settings** window:

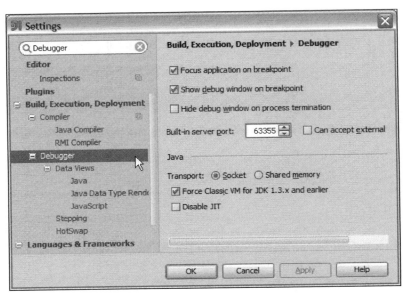

Depending on the number of enabled plugins, you will find language-specific debugger options here. Most of the options are configured properly out of the box to enable convenient debugging. You can tweak them according to your liking. Let's look at the available common options in detail now.

In the root page of the debugger settings, there are some general debugger options.

The **Transport** section will define the connection method of the process being debugged. If you are using Windows, the available values for the transport will include **Shared memory**:

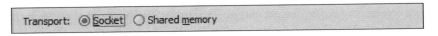

The **Shared memory** section will be faster, but the **Socket** transport has an advantage — the debugger will use the same universal debugging protocol on the local and remote machines. When you deploy your application to a remote server, the only evident configuration change will be the IP address.

If you happen to work on some legacy code and must use the old JDK, checking the **Force classic VM for JDK 1.3.x and earlier** option might be a good option. This is a rather rare situation, given the fact, that JDK 1.3 was put in an end-of-life state in 2007. However, if you need it, debugging using the classic VM is much faster than debugging with HotSpot under the old JDK.

Disabling JIT will basically pass `Djava.compiler=NONE` at runtime when the application is launched. This will affect the JIT compiler; if checked, the JIT compiler will be disabled.

Hide debug window on process termination will make the **Debug** tool window disappear when the debugged application terminates. It's good to have this option checked; the **Debug** window is useless if the debugger is not running, anyway.

If **Focus application on breakpoint** is selected, on hitting a breakpoint IntelliJ IDEA will show the source code containing the breakpoint in the editor. Again, I believe it's good to have it checked. After hitting the breakpoint, it will be easier to comprehend what is going on and evaluate expressions or create watches.

In the **Data Views** section, you can customize the way the data is displayed in the debugger. The options have very intuitive names:

- **Value tooltips delay (ms)**: This will control the tooltips that show the value of the variable when you hover the mouse cursor over the **Variables** tab or, in the editor, when your application is paused on a breakpoint.

- **Sort alphabetically**: This will show the nodes in alphabetical order.

- **Enable auto expressions in Variables view**: This option will force the debugger to analyze the source code near the breakpoint when stopped. It will read one statement before and one statement after the line containing the breakpoint. If there are no method invocations in the surrounding lines, the debugger will try to pick up any expression from these lines and put them in the **Variables** view. We will describe the **Variables** view later in this chapter.

In the **Java** section of **Data Views**, selecting **Autoscroll to new local variables** will make the IDE automatically scroll the list for new variables that appear in scope when stepping. **Auto tooltips for values** will make IntelliJ IDEA show the values of the variables when you hover the mouse cursor over them. The tip will present the value in an alternative (and sometimes more readable) way.

The **Show** subsection describes how the object and its properties will be presented in the debugger. This allows you to toggle between showing and hiding various elements such as static fields or object IDs, for example.

In the following screenshot of the debugger preferences, you can specify which classes should be presented by executing their `toString()` method:

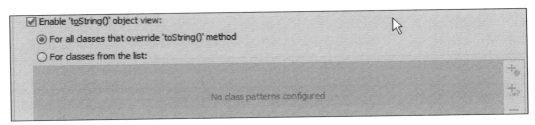

By default, IntelliJ IDEA will execute `toString()` on all classes that override the standard `toString()` method. You can customize this action by specifying your own list; use the Add class button to open the **Choose Class** dialog box or **Add Pattern** to open the Filter prompt:

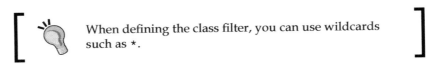

When defining the class filter, you can use wildcards such as *.

In the **Java Data Type Renderers** section, you can tweak the way different objects are displayed in the debugger. Instead of relying on the object's `String` representation, any expression can be assigned to display the object instead.

To add a new data type renderer, click on **Add**, specify its name, and define the type of objects to be affected by the renderer. This should be the fully qualified name of the class. Click on the ellipsis browse button to display the good old **Find Class** dialog box, where you can choose the desired type from the list. As always, start entering the search keywords to narrow down the list.

The data type renderers are executed twice on rendering a node in the debugger and on expanding the node, when the children information is presented. The dialog box shown in the following screenshot shows the two cases in separate radio groups:

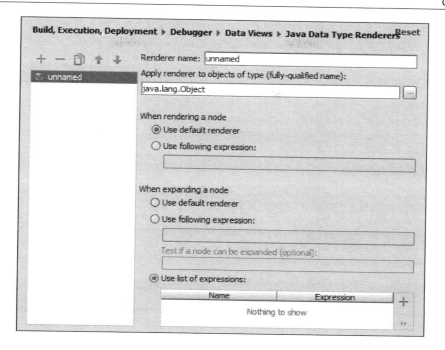

Instead of using the default renderer, you can provide your own expressions in the **Use following expression** field. In the expression fields, you can use an object's properties, constants, and String methods to construct the output.

Normally, expanding a node in the debugger lists the object's member variables by using the renderer to correct their object types. Editing the **When expanding a node** section allows you to overrule that behavior and select a single expression or a series of expressions to render the appearance. The optional **Test if the node can be expanded** field accepts a `Boolean` expression, that, if `true`, will make the IDE display the expandable nodes for the defined objects; otherwise, no nodes will be displayed. When editing the expressions, all of the code completion features are at your disposal.

When editing the expression in the data type renderer, use the keyword **this** to refer to the instance to which the renderer is going to be applied.

In the next section, **Stepping**, we can configure stepping behavior, as shown in the following screenshot. Basically, we choose what the debugger should ignore while stepping. By choosing what to skip, we can improve the debug stepping speed.

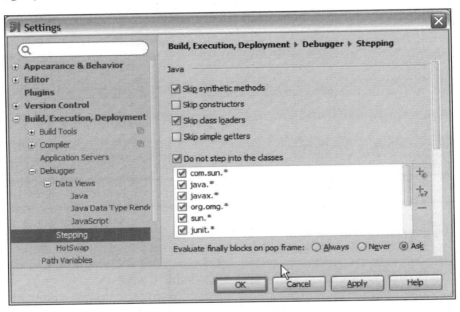

The **Skip synthetic methods** will convert stepping into methods generated by the compiler. The **Skip constructors**, **Skip class loaders**, and **Skip simple getters** option names are pretty self-explanatory; they will make the debugger ignore constructors, class loaders, and access methods accordingly.

In the **Do not step into the classes** list, you can add custom classes that should be ignored. The list of classes contains two types of entries: fully qualified class names and class patterns.

You can include or exclude specific packages by modifying the checkboxes selection. By default, the list contains some standard Java SDK and IntelliJ IDEA runtime class patterns, so you can save some of your time by not stepping onto them. Use the checkboxes in the list to disable/enable particular patterns. Use the Add Class, Add Package, and Add Pattern buttons to manage the list.

Stepping can be configured for JavaScript as well. Tick the corresponding checkboxes to force IntelliJ IDEA to ignore the JavaScript library and other specified scripts when stepping, as shown in the following screenshot:

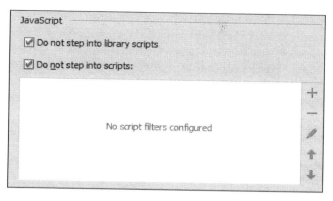

Use the **Hotswap** page to manage the behavior of the Java HotSwap mechanism. The components of the **Hotswap** page are explained in more detail in the following points:

- If **Make project before reloading classes** is turned on and you select **Reload Changed Classes** form the **Run** menu, the make process will be performed first.

- If you check the **Enable "JVM will hang" warning** checkbox and try to perform the HotSwap operation while the application is suspended, IntelliJ IDEA will produce a warning about the possible freezing of the Java Virtual Machine. It's better to have this option checked.

- Select **Reload classes in background** to reload classes and their process in the background; all progress messages will be displayed in IntelliJ IDEA's status bar.

- The section **Reload classes after compilation** controls how the HotSwap mechanism should behave. **Always** will reload classes automatically, **Never** will basically turn HotSwap off, and **Ask** will make IntelliJ IDEA prompt you whether to reload the changed classes or not.

 Hot swapping is doable only if a method body is altered. If a method or class signature has changed, the class reload will not be possible. There is a commercial plugin named JRebel that allows us to reload almost every change at runtime.

We covered the setting up of the Java debugger. In the next section, we will focus on the JavaScript debugger.

Setting up the JavaScript debugger

Web applications are probably the most popular application type nowadays. If you work on the frontend, JavaScript debugging can come in handy. Of course, the JavaScript Developer Tools included in Chrome or Firefox's Firebug are very, very good. However, having a common IDE with a powerful editor, refactoring tools, and keyboard shortcuts to debug the backend and frontend at the same time will boost your productivity a lot without question. IntelliJ IDEA comes equipped with a fully featured JavaScript debugger. It's bundled as a JetBrains plugin and is enabled by default. If you happen to disable it, refer the *Picking your plugins* section in *Chapter 1, Get to Know Your IDE, Fast*, to enable it again.

You can install additional plugins to support JavaScript libraries such as AngularJS to get the code completion and hints in the editor.

The JavaScript debugger in IntelliJ IDEA communicates with the browser; it can be either Chrome or Firefox. Before you start the debugger, you will need to install the extension for these browsers to enable this communication. For Chrome, head to Chrome Web Store and search for the **JetBrains IDE Support** extension, as shown in the following screenshot, and then install it:

When it comes to Firefox, if you start the debugging session for the first time and have configured Firefox as a browser of your choice in the run/debug configuration profile, IntelliJ IDEA will display a prompt for you to install the add-on for the browser, as shown here:

Click on **OK** and then accept the request to install third-party add-ons in the browser. Firefox will restart and communicate with the IDE.

During a debugging session, IntelliJ IDEA will use the port specified in **Built-in server port** to communicate with the Chrome extension or Firefox add-on. It's provided by default, but you can specify another value in the **Debugger** settings as shown here:

If the port is already taken, the IDE will find the closest available port and display its value, as shown in the following screenshot:

You can also specify the port value manually. In both cases, you will need to adjust the port number in the browser extension settings; otherwise, the IDE will not be able to communicate with the browser and will report the following error:

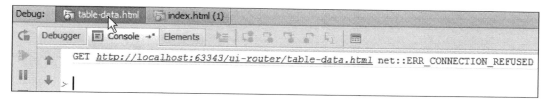

The **Selecting Show DOM** properties window will make the IDE display the DOM properties in the **Variables** pane of the **Debug** tool window if you use Firefox. We will describe the **Variables** tab later in this chapter. If you are using Chrome, the DOM properties will be displayed in the **Elements** tab.

By selecting **Show function values**, you force the IDE to display the values of functions under the **Functions** node in the **Variables** tab. Showing only the user-defined functions will limit the list to your own functions only.

If you want IntelliJ IDEA to show certain object properties in the **Variables** tab, add them to the **Show the following properties for an object node** list. The **Variables** tab will display a label with the values of the listed properties. A good candidate to add to the list is Angular's $id property, for example.

If you want the IDE to ignore specified scripts or libraries during the debugger stepping, add them to the list using the **Do not step into library scripts** and **Do not step into scripts** checkboxes in the **Debugger** section of the **Settings** dialog box.

Now, if we have the JavaScript debugger set up and are able to communicate with the browser, we can move on. From now on, we will debug in Java, but most of the topics we are going to explain will be the same for all the supported languages: setting breakpoints, adding watches, and evaluating the expressions. Let's place some traps in the code—the breakpoints.

Managing breakpoints

There are a couple of breakpoint types in IntelliJ IDEA: the line, exception, field, and method breakpoints. Let's start with the most common type: the line breakpoint.

The line breakpoints are placed on the gutter. We described the gutter in the very first chapter. To position the breakpoint, simply click on the gutter where you want the debugger to stop. You can also use the *Ctrl + F8* (PC) or *cmd + F8* (Mac) keyboard shortcut. The selected line will be shaded in red and the big red dot on the gutter will represent the breakpoint as shown here:

```java
@Override
public void setUserData(JsonObject userData) {
    try {
        currentUser = objectReader.readValue(userData.encode());
    } catch (IOException e) {
        logger.error("Error reading user data", e);
    }
}
```

> Line breakpoints can be set on executable lines only. Comments, declarations, and blank lines are not suitable locations for line breakpoints.

Another type of breakpoint is the method breakpoint; it lets you follow the program flow at the method level. To set the breakpoint on the method, just click on the gutter near the method signature as shown in the following screenshot:

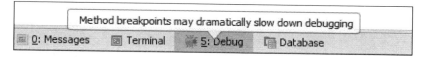

```java
private void addOrCreateRef(Resource.Method webMethod, String name, Method serviceMethod) {
    if (serviceMethods.containsKey(webMethod)) {
        serviceMethods.get(webMethod).put(name, serviceMethod);
    } else {
        HashMap<String, Method> serviceMethodNameValueMap = new HashMap<>();
        serviceMethodNameValueMap.put(name, serviceMethod);
        serviceMethods.put(webMethod, serviceMethodNameValueMap);
    }
}
```

Be warned, however, that the method breakpoint will slow down the debugging process a lot. IntelliJ IDEA will warn you about this as shown here:

Method breakpoints may dramatically slow down debugging

☰ 0: Messages   ▣ Terminal   ⚫ 5: Debug   ▦ Database

The reason for this slowdown is that the Java runtime has to add checks on every method entry to check whether it matches the breakpointed method signature. Also, the method inlining (an optimization performed by the Java **Just-In-Time** (**JIT**) compiler) becomes impossible; small methods will run 10 to 100 times more slowly.

If you notice that the debugging session is very slow, you may have some method breakpoints set up by accident. You can review, disable, or delete active breakpoints in the **Breakpoints** dialog box. We will discuss this dialog box in a minute.

If you would like the debugger to stop at a method, consider placing the ordinary line breakpoint on the first line of the method instead of using the method breakpoint.

 To move a breakpoint, just drag a line breakpoint to the needed line. The field/method breakpoint can be dragged as well, but to another field/method declaration only.

To delete the breakpoint, simply click on it or use the *Ctrl + F8* (PC) or *cmd + F8* (Mac) keyboard shortcut again.

To change the breakpoint state from active to disabled, put the caret on the line with the breakpoint and select **Toggle Breakpoint Enabled** from the **Run** menu, as shown here:

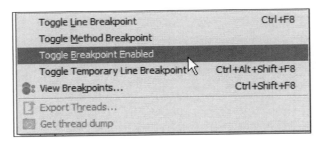

Alternatively, you can right-click on the breakpoint with your mouse, uncheck the first checkbox in the pop-up dialog box, and click on **Done** as shown here:

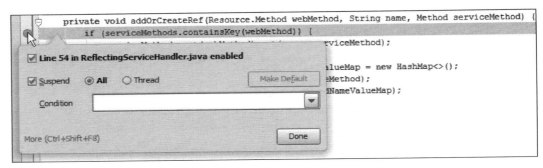

The breakpoint icon on the gutter will turn green. This means that the breakpoint is now disabled. The disabled breakpoint will no longer stop the debugger, as can be observed from the following screenshot:

```
        private void addOrCreateRef(Resource.Method webMethod, String name, Method serviceMethod) {
            if (serviceMethods.containsKey(webMethod)) {
                serviceMethods.get(webMethod).put(name, serviceMethod);
            } else {
                HashMap<String, Method> serviceMethodNameValueMap = new HashMap<>();
                serviceMethodNameValueMap.put(name, serviceMethod);
                serviceMethods.put(webMethod, serviceMethodNameValueMap);
            }
        }
```

 You can toggle the breakpoint state between enabled and disabled by clicking on it using the mouse with the *Alt* key pressed.

Sometimes you would like to stop once and investigate the problem without being bothered with the active breakpoint set up in the code. There is a nice feature in IntelliJ IDEA named temporary breakpoints. A temporary breakpoint will be removed when hit. To place a temporary breakpoint, use **Toggle Temporary Line Breakpoint** from the **Run** menu. Alternatively, you can place an ordinary line breakpoint, then click on it with the right mouse button, select **Remove once hit**, and then click on **Done**:

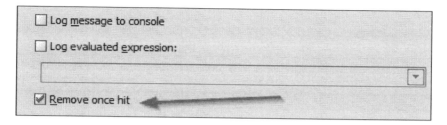

The temporary line breakpoint will be represented with a red icon containing the number **1** inside as shown here:

If you want the debugger to stop if a specific instance variable field is being accessed or modified, use **Field Watchpoint**. This is a special kind of breakpoint that will pause the execution if any access or modification to the instance variable is being made.

To create **Field Watchpoint**, place the caret in the line with the field definition and place the breakpoint in the usual way, either by clicking on the gutter or by using the *Ctrl + F8* (PC) or *cmd + F8* (Mac) keyboard shortcut. The Field Watchpoint will be represented with a slightly different gutter icon as shown here:

You can enable or disable a Field Watchpoint the same way as the other breakpoints, by clicking on it using the mouse with the *Alt* key pressed. Disabled Field Watchpoints will also turn green as shown here:

```
        private BillValidatorService billValidatorService;
```

The line/method breakpoints and Field Watchpoints can be set from the editor. If you want to tweak their behavior or define breakpoints of different types, you will need to open the **Breakpoints** dialog box. To do this, use **View Breakpoints** from the **Run** menu or use the *Ctrl + Shift + F8* (PC) or *cmd + Shift + F8* (Mac) keyboard shortcut. The output is shown in the following screenshot:

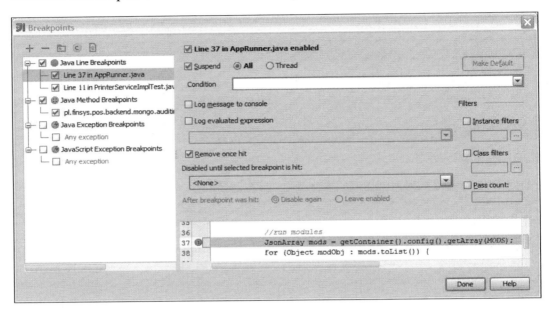

You can also access the **Breakpoints** dialog box by right-clicking on the breakpoint and selecting **More**. The keyboard shortcut for this (shown in the following screenshot) is the same as the global **View Breakpoints** command; that is, *Ctrl + Shift + F8* (PC) or *cmd + Shift + F8* (Mac):

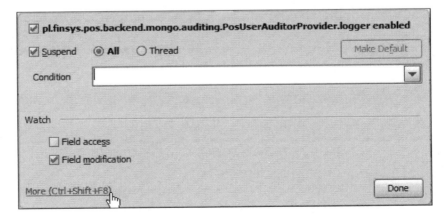

On the left side of the **Breakpoints** dialog box, you can see all breakpoints currently defined in the project. For each individual breakpoint in the list, you can view and change its properties as required. Do this by selecting the breakpoint and adjusting its options on the right side of the dialog box.

 To navigate to the breakpoints source code from the Breakpoints dialog box, double-click on the desired breakpoint, or press the F4 keyboard shortcut and close the window using *Esc*.

For every defined breakpoint, you can configure the suspend policy, as shown in the following screenshot. It defines whether the application should be suspended on hitting the breakpoint:

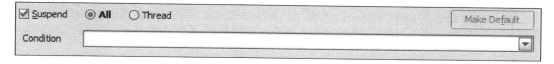

If you select **All**, all threads will be suspended when a breakpoint is hit. On the other hand, if **Thread** is selected, only the thread where the breakpoint is hit will be suspended. If the **Suspend** checkbox is not selected, no threads will be suspended.

The actions that can be performed on hitting the breakpoint include logging the message or logging the evaluated expression to the console. To log the message, mark the corresponding checkboxes. Even if the expression field is just a single line, it's equipped with all the benefits of IntelliJ IDEA's editor such as hints and parameter completion, as shown in the following screenshot:

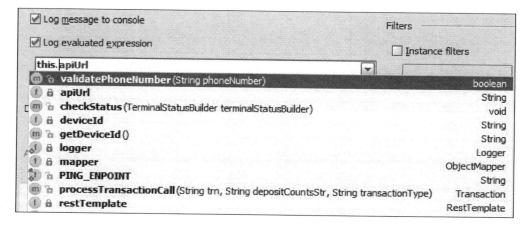

By switching off suspension and logging the message or the expression to the console, the debugger can provide you with some useful debugging information, without even stopping at the breakpoint. This is particularly useful for remote debugging situations, where you may not change the source code to add log statements to the code.

At any time, you can hover the mouse pointer in the editor over the defined breakpoint to quickly get the information about the suspend policy and actions to be executed when the breakpoint is hit, as shown in the following screenshot:

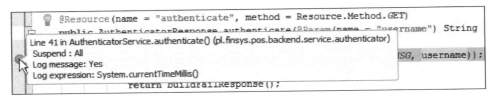

In the **Condition** field, you can enter a Java Boolean expression that should be valid in the line where the breakpoint is set. Again, the expression field contains a fully featured, syntax-aware editor. The expression is evaluated every time the breakpoint is reached. The expression can include calls to the methods that return `Boolean` values. If the evaluation result of the expression is `true`, the actions you selected will be performed. Otherwise, if the result is `false`, this breakpoint will not produce any effect and the debugger will just skip it.

Apart from providing the **Condition** expression, another way to create a conditional breakpoint is to select other breakpoints from the **Disabled until selected breakpoint is hit** drop-down list as shown here:

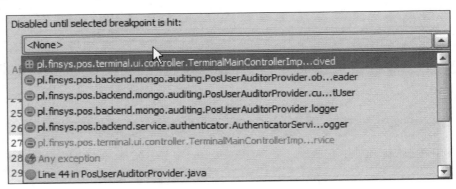

Picking any breakpoint from the list will disable the breakpoint conditionally. The breakpoint will become enabled when any other one is hit. If the breakpoint is hit, it can be disabled conditionally again or left enabled, as shown here:

The breakpoint defined this way will be presented with the conditional icon in the gutter as shown here:

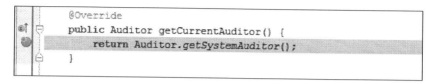

You can limit breakpoint hits only with particular object instances using their IDs. The instance ID is the Java object ID that uniquely identifies an object in the target JVM and is reported by the JVM itself. IntelliJ IDEA uses it to display variables with the @ character. For `foo.bar.MyClass@418`, the instance ID will be `418`, for example. By turning on **Instance filters** and providing ID values, you can make this breakpoint active only for specific object instances.

To filter breakpoint behavior with regard to a particular class, select the **Class filter** checkbox. Use the **Class Filters** dialog box (shown in the following screenshot) to configure class filters that determine which classes a specific breakpoint will be triggered in and in which classes it should not:

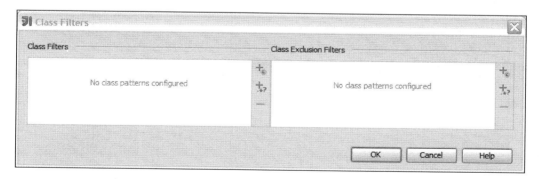

You specify classes and class patterns to be included on the left pane, and classes and class patterns to exclude on the right pane. To add a class to either of the lists, press the Add class button to open the **Choose Class** dialog box.

The filter specified through a class name points at the class itself as well as at all its subclasses.

Alternatively, to add a class pattern use the Add Pattern button. IntelliJ IDEA will show the prompt for the class pattern. The pattern may start or end with an asterisk (*), which stands for any number (including zero) of characters. A filter specified through a class pattern points at the classes whose fully qualified names match the pattern. The subclasses are selected only if their fully qualified names also match the pattern.

 The class patterns are matched against fully qualified class names.

The last option, **Pass count**, especially useful when debugging long loops, allows you to specify the counter. On each breakpoint hit, the counter will be decreased; after the specified number of passes, the execution will be suspended. In other words, this defines the number of times a breakpoint is reached but ignored. While this may be occasionally useful, it can be emulated by using the breakpoint condition expression, which is faster to use than digging through a lot of nested dialog boxes. The **Pass count** option is available only if **Instance Filters** and **Class Filters** are not marked as active.

All the breakpoints in the **Breakpoints** dialog box (shown in the following screenshot) are grouped by their type. You can group them additionally using switches in the upper toolbar. Grouping by package, class, or file is possible. To use specific grouping, just left-click on the icon.

Yet another type of breakpoint you can define is **Java Exception Breakpoint**. The debugger will stop if the exception of a specified type is thrown. This kind of breakpoint is not related to a specific source code line, but applies globally to the runtime environment. To add an exception breakpoint, click on the green plus icon in the upper toolbar, or as usual use the *Alt + Insert* keyboard shortcut to display a list of breakpoint types you can create, as shown in the following screenshot:

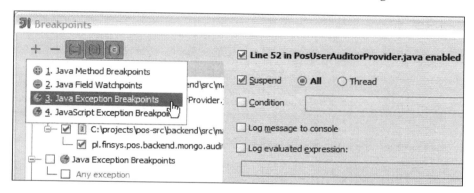

Select **Java Exception Breakpoints** from the list or use the *Alt + 3* keyboard shortcut. The well-known **Select Exception Class** dialog box will pop up, allowing you to specify the exception class from the project classpath or project. As usual, start typing to narrow down the list, as shown in the following screenshot:

To define a **Field watchpoint** using the **Breakpoints** dialog box, again use the *Alt + Insert* keyboard shortcut and select **Java Field Watchpoints** from the list this time. In the next dialog box, type the fully qualified name of the class containing the desired instance variable. Alternatively, you can use *Shift + Enter* to search for the class using the well-known class finder dialog box. When the name of the class in filled, type the name of the instance variable or press *Shift + Enter* again to display the list of instance variables to choose from, as shown in the following screenshot:

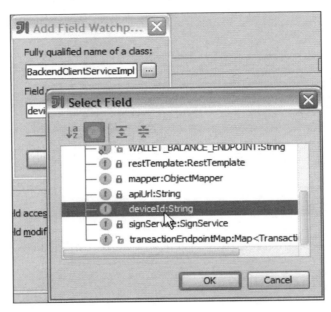

If you click on **OK**, by default the field will be monitored for modification only. You can change this behavior and make IntelliJ IDEA watch for access fields as well; just select the appropriate checkbox as shown here:

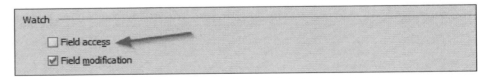

Field watchpoints can be created from the **Debug** tool window as well. We will discuss this process later in this chapter.

The list of breakpoints is also visible in the **Favorites** tool window. If you want the list to be visible all the time, just pin the tool window, as we described in the first chapter. The icons in the tool window are the same as in the gutter to easily distinguish the breakpoint's type. To remove the breakpoint or field watchpoint, select it from the list and click on the minus icon; or use **Delete** from the context menu.

In the editor, locate the line with the watchpoint or breakpoint to be deleted and click on its icon in the gutter. You can also remove the breakpoint using the **Breakpoints** dialog box. Additionally, you can remove all breakpoints of a certain type; just select the whole group and execute the **Delete** action.

Now that we have our breakpoints explained and set, let's see how they work in real life. Let's start the debugger session.

Starting the debugger

To begin the debugging session, you will need the runtime/debug configuration defined for the project. We described this process in detail in *Chapter 5, Make It Happen – Running Your Project*. This time, though, instead of running the defined configuration, use the *Shift + F9* (PC) or *Ctrl + D* (Mac) keyboard shortcut; or click on the **Debug** icon on the toolbar, as shown here:

When you start the debug configuration, two things will happen. First, IntelliJ IDEA will analyze the breakpoints you set up and, if they are valid, will mark them with the valid breakpoint icon, as shown here:

```
private void go() {
    //test comment
    String[] test = new String[] { "a", "b", "c"};
    for (int i = 0; i < test.length; i++) {
```

Otherwise, if the breakpoint is invalid, the IDE will mark it with the invalid breakpoint icon and thus ignore it. The breakpoint can be invalid because it is placed on the line with the comment or in a block with an opening or closing brace, for example, as shown here:

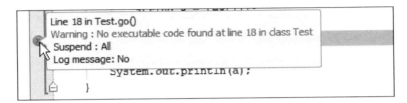

Hover over the invalid breakpoint to see the reason why IntelliJ IDEA decided not to take it into account:

The validity of the breakpoints is presented only when the debugger session is started and active.

The second thing that will happen is that the **Debug** tool window becomes available; let's focus on it as shown in the following screenshot:

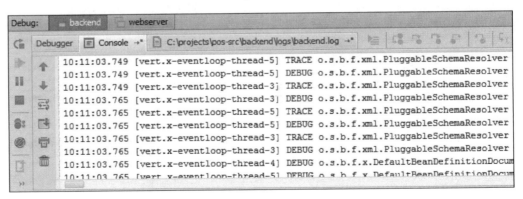

The Debug tool window

If you are debugging multiple applications at once by executing multiple debug configurations, each one will display its output in a separate tab. The tab will be named after the corresponding debug configuration is executed.

By default, the **Debug** tool window will switch itself to the **Console** tab and display the output generated by your application. If the debugger stops, the most interesting stuff can be performed on the first tab: the **Debugger** tab. Let's take a closer look at it now.

You will find three nested tabs here that present the current state of the suspended application: **Frames**, **Variables**, and **Watches** as shown here:

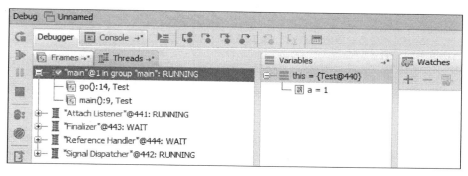

You can hide unnecessary tabs by using the hide icon in the tab itself as shown here:

The hidden tab can then be restored using its icon in the Hide/Restore toolbar, available in the upper-right corner of the **Debug** tool window. You can toggle the additional **Threads** tab as well, as shown in the following screenshot:

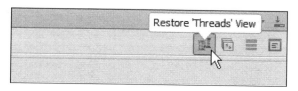

Let's discuss the tabs in detail. The **Frames** and **Threads** tabs are very similar. They both give you access to the list of frames and threads in your application. A frame corresponds to an active method or function call. A frame stores the local variables of the method or function called, its arguments, and the code context that enables evaluation of the expressions.

In the **Frames** pane, you select the thread you are interested in from the drop-down list as shown here:

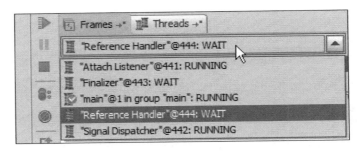

To navigate between frames, use the up and down arrow buttons on the toolbar or the up arrow and down arrow keys on the keyboard.

The **Threads** tab, for a change, shows all the threads of a process as a tree view, presenting the name, ID, and thread status, as shown in the following screenshot:

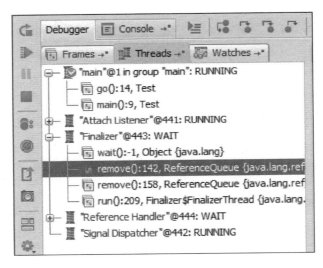

If you expand a single thread branch and click on it (in the **Frames** tab) or double-click (in the **Threads** tab) on the method name, the corresponding source code of the method will be opened in the editor. At any time, the thread view can be customized a little by right-clicking anywhere in the **Frames** or **Threads** tab and selecting **Customize Threads View** from the context menu, as shown here:

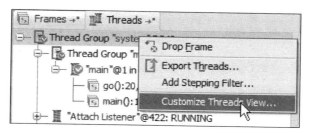

In **Customize Threads View** you can turn on some additional information to be shown, such as displaying thread groups or source file names as shown here:

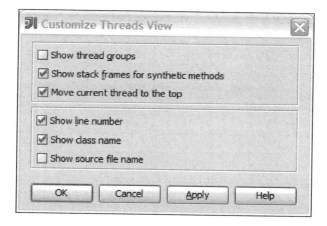

The currently suspended thread is marked with a red tick icon in the call stack. You can interrupt it by selecting **Interrupt** from the context menu. If you select the method currently being executed (and paused at the breakpoint), you can also drop a frame from the call stack using the context menu, as shown here:

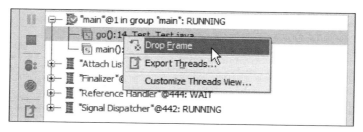

By using the **Drop Frame** functionality, you can "fall back" on the previous stack frame, in a way going back in time. You need to be aware that changes that were already made to the global state (such as static variables) and variables outside the stack frame will not be reverted. Only local variables will be reset. Dropping the frame is a useful feature to explore different paths of execution, without having to restart the application, or a particular lengthy process that led to the current stack.

Dropping a frame is very helpful to re-enter a method if you missed a critical spot.

During the debugging session, the most used functionality is inspecting variables and evaluating expressions. Let's cover that process now in more detail.

Inspecting variables and evaluating expressions

During the debugging session, IntelliJ IDEA will present the values of the variables in the editor itself, next to the variable usage, as shown in the following screenshot:

While this may be useful as a quick overview for the current state, the **Variables** tab gives you the opportunity to examine the values of the variables in your application in more detail. When a stack frame is selected in the **Frames** tab, the **Variables** tab displays all the variables within its scope, such as method parameters, and local and instance variables. Variable here are listed with their unique internal IDs we mentioned earlier; you can use this ID to define the breakpoint instance filter. Each variable in the tab has a context menu when you right-click on it as shown in the following screenshot:

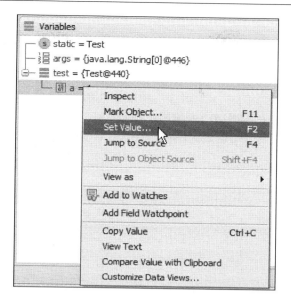

The **Set Value** option allows changing the variable value. **Inspect**, available for fields, local variables, and reference expressions, will display and track its reference in its own window:

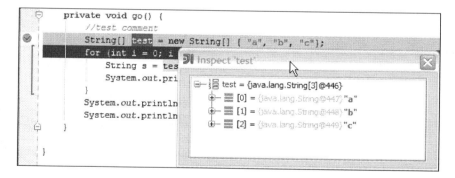

If you need to examine several references in detail, you can open an inspection window for each one of them. A separate window is created for each reference and all of its child references. All changes of the references are immediately reflected in the inspection window.

The inspection window is not modal and you can open as many as you want.

Most of the options in this context menu are self-explanatory. You can copy a variable's value to the clipboard, compare the value with the clipboard, or set the variable value. If you want to label the selected variable with a meaningful name, use the **Mark Object** command.

Pick **Customize Data Views** from the context menu as shown here:

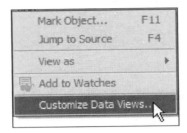

You will be presented with a dialog box containing two tabs, **Data Views** and **Data Type Renderers**, as shown in the following screenshot:

The contents of the two tabs will be the same as we described in the *Debugger settings* section at the beginning of this chapter.

If you want to evaluate a number of variables or expressions in the context of the current frame and view all of them simultaneously, you can create watches for them. The values of the expressions are updated with each step through the application, but are only visible when the application is suspended.

By using the **Add to Watches** command, you can send the selected object to the **Watches** tab. You can achieve the same effect by right-clicking on the variable in the editor and selecting **Add to Watches** from the context menu, as shown in the following screenshot:

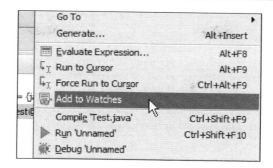

There is one important difference, though: the **Variables** tab is active only when the debugger session is running. On the other hand, the context menu in the editor is active whether the debugger session is active or not.

All the variables you added to watches will show up in the **Watches** tab, as shown in the following screenshot:

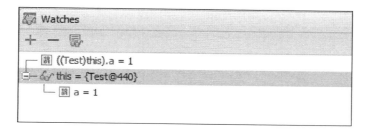

To add an item to the **Watches** pane, you can also click on the green plus icon in the toolbar; or, as always, use the *Alt + Insert* keyboard shortcut. To change the expression represented by a watch, right-click on the desired watch and select **Edit** in the context menu.

The expression field is, again, a fully featured advanced source code editor with code completion and hints available, as shown here:

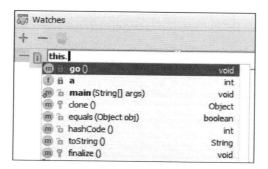

To remove a watch, select it in the **Watches** pane and choose **Remove Watch** from the context menu or use the *Delete* key.

The **Watches** tab context menu has very similar functionality to the one present in the **Variables** tab. Additionally, you can use it to edit the watch, remove the watch, or remove all watches, as shown here:

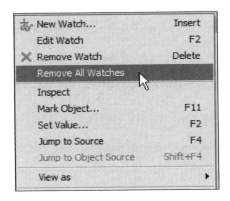

 Watches are persisted as part of a project. They will be preserved if you close the project.

Apart from creating watches, you can also define field watchpoints in the **Variables** tab. Just select the variable and choose **Add Field Watchpoint** to have a breakpoint defined as shown in the following screenshot:

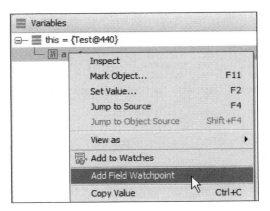

Probably the most often used feature of the debugger is the expression evaluation. Apart from having values of the variables presented in the **Variables** or **Watches** tab, you will often evaluate expressions on-the-fly. The IDE enables you to evaluate an arbitrary expression from the context of the stack frame currently selected in the **Frames** tab. The following modes are available: **Expression Mode** to evaluate single-line expressions and **Code Fragment Mode** to evaluate short code blocks, including declarations, assignments, if/else constructs, and loops.

IntelliJ IDEA provides a way to quickly evaluate an expression at the caret or a selection. If the debugger stops on the breakpoint, select the variable or expression you want to evaluate and start the **Evaluate Expression** dialog box (shown in the following screenshot) by choosing the **Evaluate Expression** command from the **Run** menu or using the *Alt + F8* (PC) or *option + F8* (Mac) keyboard shortcut:

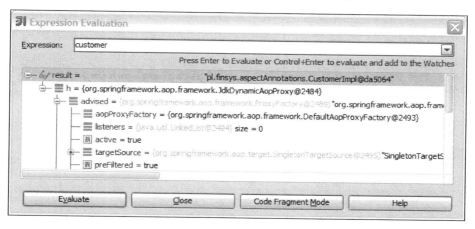

Expression mode is active by default; if you want to evaluate a code fragment, click on the **Code Fragment Mode** button, the result of which is shown in the following screenshot:

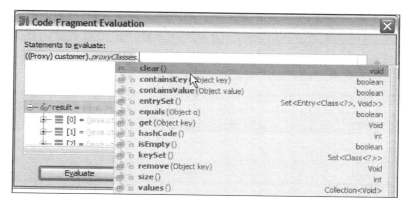

As you will quickly find out, the expression field comes with all the benefits of the IntelliJ IDEA source code editor. You will find syntax highlighting, code completion, hints, and every powerful feature the IDE has to offer in terms of editing code. You can even use live templates here, as we described in *Chapter 3, The Editor*.

 A method can be invoked within the **Expression Evaluation** dialog box only if the debugger has stopped at a breakpoint, but has not been paused manually.

Take note that, if a method invoked within **Expression Evaluation** has a breakpoint inside its body, this breakpoint will be ignored.

If the specified expression cannot be evaluated, IntelliJ IDEA will describe the reason in a few words in the **Result** pane of the dialog box as shown here:

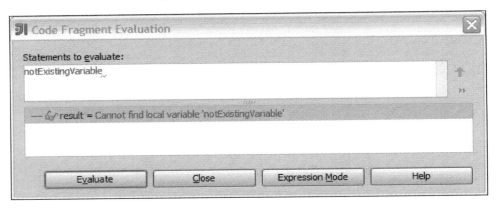

If you are using the mouse during the development process, you can quickly evaluate the value of any expression by placing the mouse cursor over the expression during the debugger session. The value of the expression will be shown as a tooltip, as shown in the following screenshot:

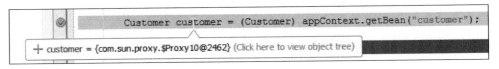

If an expression contains children, clicking on the green plus icon will expand the hint in the object tree dialog box and display all of the children.

Clicking on the variable in the editor with the left *Alt* key pressed will show the dialog box with the expression value evaluated.

Apart from the Hide/Restore toolbar, the **Debug** tool window has two toolbars of great importance: the **Debug** toolbar and the **Stepping** toolbar. We will explore them now.

Debugger actions

All of the actions available in the toolbars mimic the actions present in the **Run** menu during the debugging session. I believe that using the toolbars is more convenient than using the menu (apart from using keyboard shortcuts, of course). Let's take a look at them now.

The Debug toolbar contains actions to manage your debugging session. You can restart the debugging session by using the *Ctrl + F5* (PC) or *option + F5* (Mac) keyboard shortcut. If the session is stopped, this command will turn in to the Debug button, which will start the debugging session again, as shown here:

When an application is paused, you can click on the Resume Program button, or use the *F9* (PC) or *cmd + Option + R* (Mac) keyboard shortcut, to resume the program execution, as shown here:

Click on the Pause button to suspend the execution and the Stop button to stop
the debugging session, as shown here:

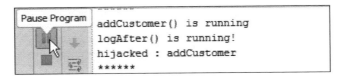

There is a useful button you can use to temporarily disable all the defined
breakpoints: the Mute Breakpoints button (shown in the following screenshot). Use
this to change the status of the breakpoints from enabled to disabled and vice versa.
With breakpoints muted, the program will execute without stopping.

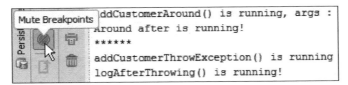

The Get thread dump button will allow you to review the thread dump in a
convenient and readable way. The tab is divided into two parts: the left one displays
all the threads and the right one displays the stack trace for the selected thread,
as shown here:

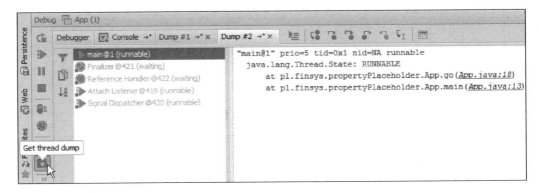

The stepping toolbar contains commands to navigate the execution flow during
the debugging session. The first one is Show Execution Point, available with
the *Alt + F10* (PC) or *option + F10* (Mac) keyboard shortcut, as shown in the
following screenshot:

When you go away from the point where the debugger stopped, either by switching the editor's windows or navigating to other files or methods, Show Execution Point will quickly get you back to the point of interest, which is the current execution point where you can continue stepping.

The Step Over command (the *F8* keyboard shortcut) will make the debugger run until the next line in the current method or file. If the current line is the last one in the method, execution shifts to the line executed right after this method.

The Step Into command (the *F7* keyboard shortcut) will make the debugger step inside the method called at the current execution point. If the method is set to be skipped in the Stepping page in the Debugger settings dialog box, as we described at the beginning of this chapter, you can use the Force Step Into command or the *Alt + Shift + F7* (PC) or *option + Shift + F7* (Mac) keyboard shortcut. The Force Step Into command permits you to dig into a class from the list of classes not to be stepped into; for example, a standard Java SDK class. Clicking on the Step Out command (the *Shift + F8* keyboard shortcut), will make the debugger step out of the current method, to the line executed right after the execution of this method. One feature I find especially useful is Run to Cursor, shown in the following screenshot:

This action will resume program execution and pause until the flow reaches the line at the cursor position in the editor. You don't need to define the breakpoint for this. It's like a temporary breakpoint defined implicitly. Be aware that, if the cursor is positioned on the line that has already been executed, the execution flow will just be resumed, and you will have no chance to go back.

When you have stepped too deep into the method's sequence and need to step out of several methods at once, use the Run to Cursor feature.

Now you know how to navigate within the debugger. Let's make it even faster and more effective by summarizing keyboard shortcuts worth using while debugging.

Keyboard shortcuts summary

The following table summarizes debugger actions and associated shortcuts:

Action	PC shortcut	Mac shortcut
Debug	*Shift + F9*	*control + D*
Step over	*F8*	*F8*
Force step over	*Alt + Shift + F8*	*option + Shift + F8*
Step into	*F7*	*F7*
Force step into	*Alt + Shift + F7*	*option + Shift + F7*
Run to cursor	*Alt + F9*	*option + F9*
Evaluate expression	*Alt + F8*	*option + F8*
Resume program	*F9*	*cmd + option + R*
Toggle breakpoint	*Ctrl + F8*	*cmd + F8*
View breakpoints	*Ctrl + Shift + F8*	*cmd + Shift + F8*
Show execution point	*Alt + F10*	*option + F10*

Summary

As you can see, debugging in IntelliJ IDEA is very handy. After reading this chapter, you know how to set up the debugger, place and manage the breakpoints, and look under the hood (that is, inspecting variables, adding and tracking watches, and evaluating expressions). Searching for bugs will be easy and effective.

You now know how to set up a project and unleash the power of the state-of-the art code editor. You can define a runtime or debug configuration to execute the application. Well, this should be enough to get you going. However, there's some more — version control. You can probably work on your software in the team and use a version control system, such as SVN or GIT. Even if you work alone, having version control set up is a great idea. IntelliJ IDEA provides first-class support for a version control system such as SVN or GIT. We are going to cover this subject in the next chapter.

9
Working with Your Team

While working on the code, one of the most important aspects is version control. A **Version Control System (VCS)** (also known as a Revision Control System) is a repository of source code files with monitored access. Every change made to the source is tracked, along with who made the change, why they made it, and comments about problems fixed or enhancements introduced by the change. It doesn't matter if you work alone or in a team, having the tool to efficiently work with different versions of the code is crucial. Software development is usually carried out by teams, either distributed or colocated. The version control system lets developers work on a copy of the source code and then release their changes back to the common codebase when ready. Other developers work on their own copies of the same code at the same time, unaffected by each other's changes until they choose to merge or commit their changes back to the project. Currently, probably the most popular version control system is Git, but in this chapter, we will also talk about working with other VCS systems such as Subversion. After reading this chapter, you will be able to set up the version control mechanism of your choice, get files from the repository, commit your work, browse changes, and handle differences. Let's start with the version control setup.

Enabling version control

At the IDE level, version control integration is provided through a set of plugins. IntelliJ IDEA comes bundled with a number of plugins to integrate with the most popular version control systems. They include Git, CVS, Subversion, and Mercurial. The Ultimate edition additionally contains Clearcase, Visual SourceSafe, and Perforce plugins. You will need to enable them in the **Plugins** section of the **Settings** dialog box, as we described in *Chapter 1, Get to Know Your IDE, Fast*.

If you find the VCS feature is not enough and you are using some other VCS, try to find it in the **Browse Repositories** dialog box by choosing **VCS Integration** from the **Category** drop-down menu, as shown here:

The list of plugins here contains not only integration plugins, but also some useful add-ons for the installed integrations. For example, the **SVN Bar** plugin will create a quick access toolbar with buttons specific for **Subversion (SVN)** actions. Feel free to browse the list of plugins here and read the descriptions; you might find some valuable extensions.

The basic principles of working with the version control systems in IntelliJ IDEA are rather similar. We will focus on the Git and Subversion integration. Although the detailed explanation of working with Git and Subversion is out of the scope of this book, this chapter should give you an overview of how to deal with the setup and version control commands in IntelliJ IDEA in general. If you have the necessary plugins enabled in the **Settings** dialog box, you can start working with the version control. We will begin with fetching the project out of the version control. Doing this will set up the version control automatically so that further steps will not be required unless you decide not to use the default workflow. Later, we will cover setting the VCS integration manually, so you will be able to tweak IntelliJ's behavior then.

Checking out the project from the repository

To be able to work on the files, first you need to get them from the repository. To get the files from the remote Git repository, you need to use the `clone` command available in the **VCS** menu, under the **Checkout from Version Control** option, as shown here:

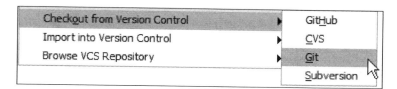

In the **Clone Repository** dialog box, provide necessary options, such as the remote repository URL, parent directory, and the directory name to clone into, as shown in the following screenshot:

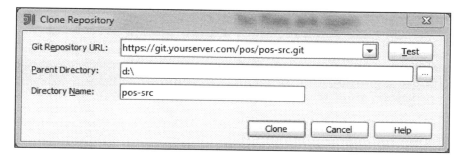

After successful cloning, IntelliJ IDEA will suggest creating a project based on the cloned sources. Refer to *Chapter 2, Off We Go – To the Code*, to find the description on how to deal with the project creation process. If you don't have the remote repository for your project, you can work with the offline local Git repository. To create a local Git repository, select **Create Git repository** from the **VCS** menu, as shown in the following screenshot:

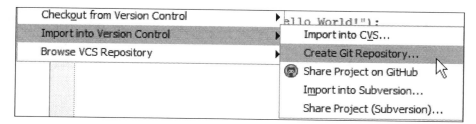

This option will execute the `git init` command in the directory of your choice; it will most probably be the root directory of your project.

For the time being, the Git plugin does not allow you to set up remote repositories. You will probably need to set up the remote host for your newly created Git repository before you can actually fetch and push changes.

> If you are using GitHub for your projects, the great GitHub integration plugin gives you the option to share the project on GitHub. This will create the remote repository automatically.

Later, when you want to get the files from the remote repository, just use the Git **Pull** command. This will basically retrieve changes (`fetch`) and apply them to the local branch (`merge`).

To obtain a local working copy of a subversion repository, choose **Checkout from Version Control** and then **Subversion** from the **VCS** menu. In the **SVN Checkout Options** dialog box, you will be able to specify Subversion-specific settings, such as a revision that needs to be checked (HEAD, for example). Again, IntelliJ IDEA will ask if you want to create the project from checked out sources. If you accept the suggestion to create a new project, **New Project from Existing Code Wizard** will start.

Fetching the project out of the repository will create some default VCS configuration in IntelliJ IDEA. It is usually sufficient, but if needed, the configuration can be changed. Let's discuss how to change the configuration in the next section.

Configuring version control

The VCS configuration in IntelliJ IDEA can be changed at the project level. Head to the **Version Control** section in the **Settings** dialog box, as shown here:

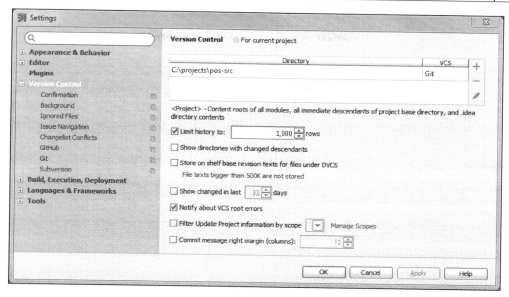

The **Version Control** section contains options that are common for all version control systems and also specific options for the different VCS systems (enabled by installing the corresponding plugins). IntelliJ IDEA uses a directory-based model for version control. The versioning mechanism is assigned to a specific directory that can either be a part of a project or can be just related to the project. This directory is not required to be located under the project root.

 Multiple directories can have different version control systems linked.

To add a directory into the version control integration, use the *Alt + Insert* keyboard shortcut or click on the green plus button; the **Add VCS Directory Mapping** dialog box will appear.

You have the option to put all the project contents, starting from its base directory to the version control or limit the version control only to specific directories. Select the VCS system you need from the **VCS** drop-down menu, as shown in the following screenshot:

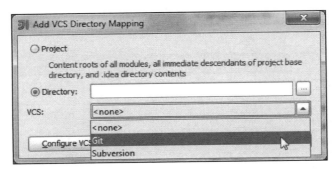

By default, IntelliJ IDEA will mark the changed files with a color in the **Project** tool window, as shown here:

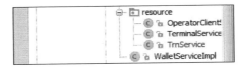

If you select the **Show directories with changed descendants** option, IntelliJ IDEA will additionally mark the directories containing the changed files with a color, giving you the possibility to quickly notice the changes without expanding the project tree, as shown in the following screenshot:

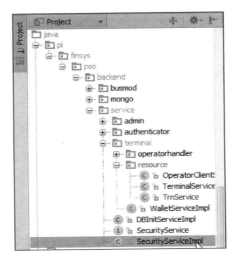

The **Show changed in last <number> days** option will highlight the files changed recently during the debugging process and when displaying stacktraces.

Displaying the changed files in color can be very useful. If you see the colored file in the stacktrace, maybe the last change to the file is causing a problem.

The subsequent panes contain general version control settings, which apply to all version control systems integrated with the IDE. They include specifying actions that require confirmation, background operations set up, the ignored files list, and issuing of navigation configuration.

In the **Confirmation** section, you specify what version control actions will need your confirmation. The **Background** section will tell IntelliJ IDEA what operation it should perform in the background, as shown in the following screenshot:

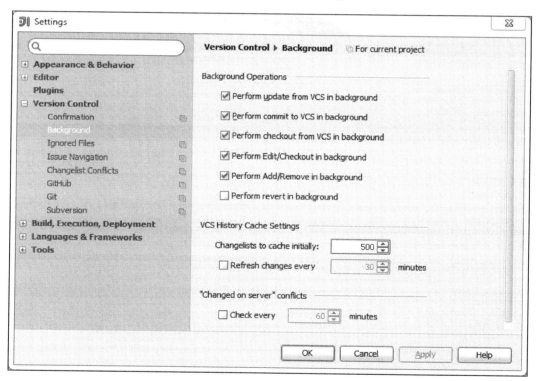

If you choose to perform the operation in the background, IntelliJ IDEA will not display any modal windows during and after the operation. The progress and result will be presented in the status bar of the IDE and in the corresponding tool windows. For example, after the successful execution of the Git `pull` command, IntelliJ IDEA will present the **Update Project Info** tool window with the files changed and the **Event Log** tool window with the status of the operation, as shown in the following screenshot:

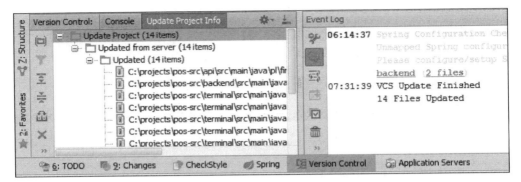

In the **Ignored Files** section, you can specify a list of files and directories that you do not want to put under version control, as shown in the following screenshot:

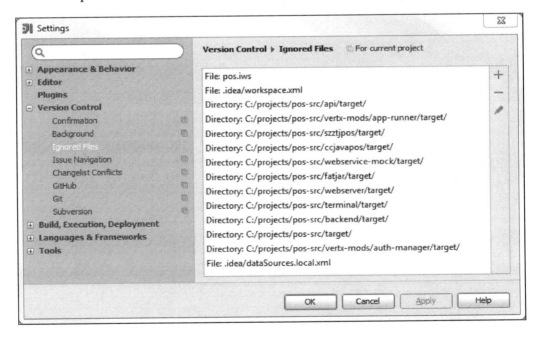

To add a file or directory, use the *Alt + Insert* keyboard shortcut or hit the green plus (**+**) icon. The **Ignore Unversioned Files** dialog box will pop up as shown here:

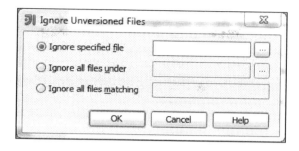

You can now specify a single file or the directory you want to ignore. There is also the possibility to construct the filename pattern for files to be ignored. Backup and logfiles are good candidates to be specified here, for example.

Most of the version control systems support the file with a list of file patterns to ignore. For Git, this will be the `.gitignore` file. IntelliJ IDEA will analyze such files during the project checkout from the existing repository and will fill the **Ignored files** list automatically.

In the **Issue Navigation** section, you can create a list of patterns to issue navigation. IntelliJ IDEA will try to use these patterns to create links from the commit messages. These links will then be displayed in the **Changes** and **Version Control** tool windows. Clicking on the link will open the browser and take you to the issue tracker of your choice. IntelliJ IDEA comes with predefined patterns for the most popular issue trackers: JIRA and YouTrack. To create a link to JIRA, click on the first button and provide the URL for your JIRA instance, as shown in the following screenshot:

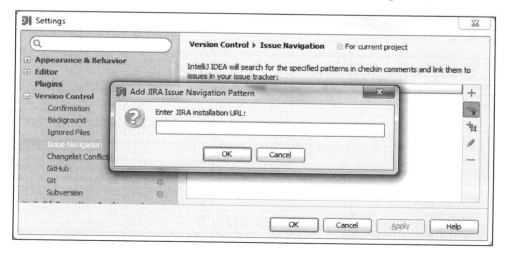

To create a link to the YouTrack instance, click on the **OK** button and provide the URL to the YouTrack instance. If you do not use JIRA or YouTrack, you can also specify a generic pattern. Press the *Alt + Insert* keyboard shortcut to add a new pattern. In the **IssueID** field, enter the regular expression that IntelliJ IDEA will use to extract a part of the link. In the **Issue Link** field, provide the link expression that IntelliJ IDEA will use to replace a issue number within. Use the **Example** section to check if the resulting link is correct, as shown in the following screenshot:

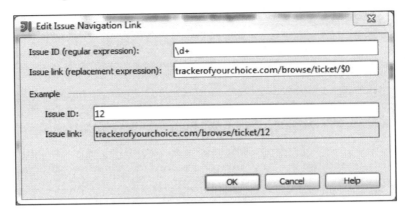

The next sections in the **Version Control** preferences list contain options specific to the version control system you are using. For example, the Git-specific options can be configured in the **Git** section, as shown here:

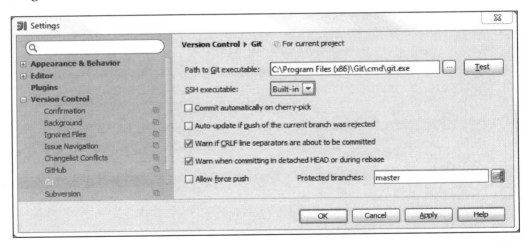

You can specify the Git command executable here or select the associated SSH executable that will be used to perform the network Git operations such as `pull` and `push`.

The **Auto-update if push of the current branch was rejected** option is quite useful—IntelliJ IDEA will execute the pull command first if the push command fails because of the changes in the repository revision. This saves some time.

We should now have version control integration up and running. Let's use it.

Working with version control

Before we start working with version control, we need to know about the concept of the changelist in IntelliJ IDEA. Let's focus on this now.

Changelists

When it comes to newly created or modified files, IntelliJ IDEA introduces the concept of a changelist. A changelist is a set of file modifications that represents a logical change in the source. Any modified file will go to the **Default** changelist. You can create new changelists if you like. The changes contained in a specific changelist are not stored in the repository until committed. Only the active changelist contains the files that are going to be committed. If you modify the file that is contained in the non-active change list, there is a risk that it will not be committed. This takes us to the last section of the common VCS settings at **Settings | Version Control | Changelist conflicts**. In this section, you can configure the protection of files that are present in the changelist that is not currently active. In other words, you define how IntelliJ IDEA should behave when you modify the file that is not in the active changelist.

The protection is turned on by default (**Enable changelist conflict tracking** is checked). If the **Resolve Changelist Conflict** checkbox is marked, the IDE will display the **Resolve Changelist Conflict** dialog box when you try to modify such a file. The possible options are to either shelve the changes (we will talk about the concept of shelving in a while), move a file to the active changelist, switch changelists to make the current changelist active, or ignore the conflict. If **Highlight files with conflicts** is checked and if you try to modify a file from the non-active change list, a warning will pop up in the editor, as shown in the following screenshot:

Again, you will have the possibility to move the changes to another change list, switch the active change list, or ignore the conflict. If you select **Ignore**, the change will be listed in the **Files with ignored conflicts** list, as shown in the following screenshot:

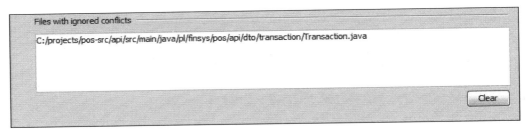

The list of all changelists in the project is listed in the **Commit Changes** dialog box (we will cover committing files in a while) and in the first tab of the **Changes** tool window, as shown here:

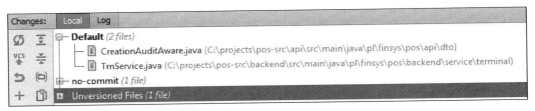

You can create a new changelist by using the *Alt + Insert* keyboard shortcut. The active list will have its name highlighted in bold. The last list is special; it contains the list of unversioned files.

 You can drag-and-drop files between the changelists (with the exception of unversioned files).

Now that we know what a changelist is, let's add some files to the repository now.

Adding files to version control

You will probably want newly created files to be placed in version control. If you create a file in a directory already associated with the version control system, IntelliJ IDEA will add the file to the active changelist automatically, unless you configured this differently in the **Confirmation** section of the **Version Control** pane in the **Settings** dialog box. If you decided to have **Show options before adding to version control** checked, IntelliJ IDEA will ask if you want to add the file to the VCS, as shown here:

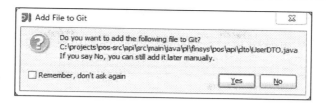

If you decide to check the **Remember, don't ask again** checkbox, IntelliJ IDEA will throw the future new files into version control silently. You can also add new files to the version control explicitly. Click on the file or directory you want to add in the **Project** tool window and choose the corresponding VCS command; for example:

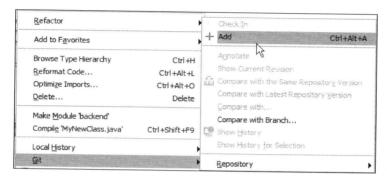

Alternatively, you can open the **Changes** tool window, and browse **Unversioned Files**, where you can right-click on the file you want to add and select **Add to VCS** from the context menu, as shown in the following screenshot:

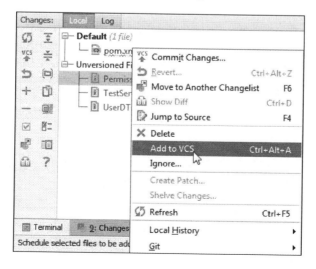

If there are many unversioned files, IntelliJ IDEA will render a link that allows you to browse the files in a separate dialog box, as shown in the following screenshot:

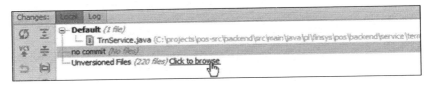

In the **Unversioned Files** dialog box, right-click on the file you want to add and select **Add to VCS** from the context menu, as shown in the following screenshot:

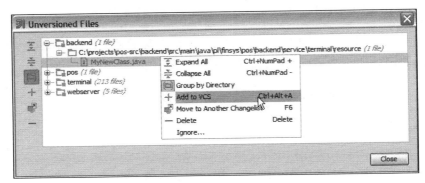

From now on, the file will be ready to commit to the repository.

 If you've accidently added some files to version control and want to change them to unversioned, you can always *revert* the file so that it is no longer marked as part of the versioned files.

Committing files

If you modify a file that is tracked by the version control mechanism, it will be marked with a color in the files tree in the project tool window, as shown in the following screenshot:

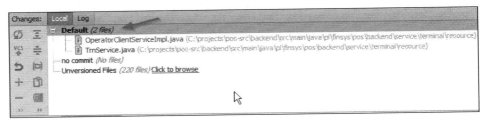

Also, the modified lines will be marked in the editor gutter, as shown here:

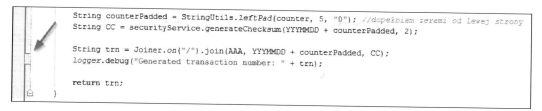

```
String counterPadded = StringUtils.leftPad(counter, 5, "0"); //dopełniam zerami od lewej strony
String CC = securityService.generateChecksum(YYYMMDD + counterPadded, 2);

String trn = Joiner.on("/").join(AAA, YYYMMDD + counterPadded, CC);
logger.debug("Generated transaction number: " + trn);

return trn;
}
```

 You can click on the colored area in the gutter to get a pop up, which shows the content in that line before it was edited. This pop up also contains a button that allows you to roll back just to change this one line.

To commit a file to the repository, use the *Ctrl + K* (PC) or *cmd + K* (Mac) keyboard shortcut. This will show the **Commit Changes** dialog box, allowing you to pick the changelist to consider and showing all modified files available to commit, as shown here:

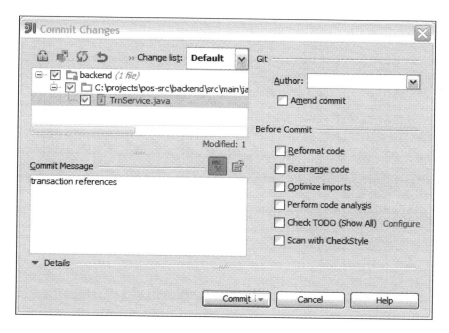

The dialog box will present all the modified and deleted files, giving you the possibility to enter a commit message. If you are using Git, you can amend the last commit by marking the **Amend commit** checkbox. This will be equivalent to the -amend Git option in the commit command.

The **Before Commit** section contains some useful, last minute actions that can be performed before a commit, such as code reformatting, optimizing Java imports, or scanning the source with a CheckStyle plugin. Every file in the **Commit Changes** dialog box has the context menu available, giving you the chance to see the difference, revert the changes, or move the change to another changelist if you decide to exclude the file from this specific commit:

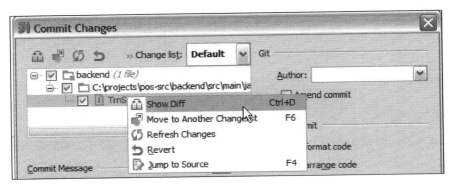

To see exactly what is going to be committed to the repository, select the file and use the *Ctrl + D* (PC) or *cmd + D* (Mac) keyboard shortcut. You will be presented with the difference screen, showing exactly the changes made to the file. We will talk about the difference viewer later in this chapter. Alternatively, you can expand the **Details** section of the **Commit Changes** dialog box to see the difference pane at the bottom, as shown in the following screenshot:

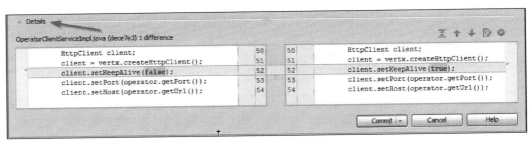

 If you don't want to commit the changes at this time, then move files to the other changelist or uncheck the checkbox before the file.

If you deleted the file that was tracked by the version control mechanism, the **Commit Changes** dialog box will list the deleted file as well with the filename grayed out. In such cases, the dialog box will also show the number of files deleted, as shown in the following screenshot:

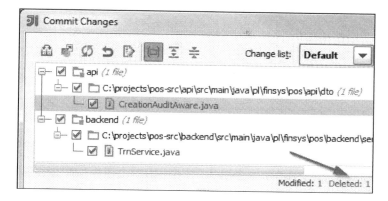

The changes will be committed if you click on the **Commit** button (the dialog box window as always supports standard shortcuts such as *Alt* + the underlined letter in the caption). If you are using Git, you can commit and push changes to the remote repository automatically. To do this, expand the **Commit** button and choose **Commit and Push**, as shown here:

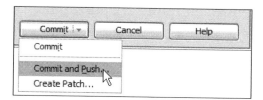

If the file you are trying to commit was modified by some other developer in the meantime, IntelliJ IDEA will display the following message saying that the commit has failed:

If you confirm the error after clicking on **OK**, the **Messages** tool window will show the explanation of the problem, in this case stating you should update first, as shown in the following screenshot:

Error: svn: E160024: Commit failed (details follow):
  svn: E160024: File or directory 'tableActions.js' is out of date; try updating
  svn: E160024: resource out of date; try updating
  svn: E175002: CHECKOUT of '/xportalen/!svn/ver/7514/branches/branch-20140925-P4920-P-laan-overdragelse

> Instead of committing the modified files, you can also create the patch file with all the changes that you have made. Expand the **Commit** button and choose **Create Patch** to be able to provide a directory name for the patch file.

At the moment, we know how to commit our modifications to the repository. Let's get the changes from the repository now.

Getting changes from the repository

To get the changes from the remote repository, execute the **Update Project** command by using the *Ctrl + T* (PC) or *cmd + T* (Mac) keyboard shortcut. If you are using Git, IntelliJ IDEA will ask how do you want the changes to be incorporated into the local working copy; it can be either Merge or Rebase. If your working copy contains pending changes, they can be put aside for a while using the Git stash command or IntelliJ IDEA's own Shelve mechanism, as shown in the following screenshot:

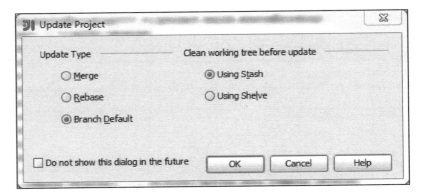

Shelving is the process of storing not yet committed changes in a dedicated "shelf". Unshelving is bringing the changes from the "shelf" back to a pending changelist, making them ready to commit. Shelving is IntelliJ IDEA's operation similar to Git `stash` with one difference: shelved changes are applied (unshelved) from within IntelliJ IDEA, as opposed to Git stashed changes, which can be applied from outside of the IDE, because they are generated by Git itself.

> When you're not using Git, shelving is a pretty nice tool to put your work in progress changes for later (such as Git stash).

When updating a project, if you are using Git, one very important feature is the ability to rebase your changes against any ref with an interactive dialog box to allow a complete reshaping of the commit history.

Mark the corresponding checkbox for not being asked for those options again and have the `pull` command be executed in the background silently.

In the case of the Subversion repository, you will be presented with the **Update Project** dialog box, where you can choose the branch or revision you want to switch to. You can also mark the **Do not show this dialog in the future** checkbox to make future project updates silent.

If the changes coming from the server are in different places than your local changes, IntelliJ IDEA will automatically merge the file. Otherwise, it will state that there is a merge conflict and give you some options, as shown in the following screenshot:

You can now either accept your changes by right-clicking the **Accept Yours** command button, it overrides the changes incoming from the VCS server, or the **Accept Theirs** command button accepts their changes, which will throw away your local changes, or right-click on the **Merge** command button. If you choose **Merge**, the three-way merge diff viewer will show up. The left pane contains your local changes and the right pane contains the changes coming from the server. In the middle pane, there is the merge result. The number of detected conflicts is shown at the bottom of the window. You must now decide what the merge result will look like. Use the icons in the gutters of the editors to copy changes from the left (your changes) or from the right (incoming changes) or remove the specific change, as shown in the following screenshot:

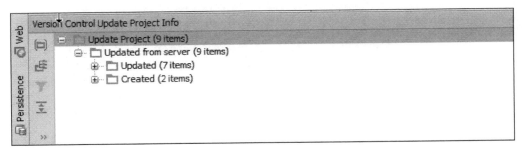

When you click on **Apply**, IntelliJ IDEA will merge the file and finish the project update.

Browsing the changes

The results of the **Update Project** action will be presented in the **Version Control** tool window at the bottom of the IDE workspace. In the following screenshot, you will see what files were updated or created in the repository since the last update:

You can expand the files tree to see individual files and use the context menu to see the differences that came from the repository. You can also press the well-known *Ctrl + D* (PC) or *cmd + D* (Mac) keyboard shortcut to show the difference window. The successful update will be noted in the status bar, as shown here:

VCS Update Finished // 6 Files Updated (moments ago)

If you update the project and there were no changes coming from the repository, IntelliJ IDEA will prompt you with a message in the status bar, as shown here:

Sometimes you decide that your changes have gone too far and would like to revert them. Let's focus on reverting the changes now.

Reverting the local changes

You can throw away your local changes in a couple of ways. The first way we already mentioned is to do it from the **Commit Changes** dialog box. Select the modified file by right-clicking on the file and select **Revert** from the context menu, as shown in the following screenshot:

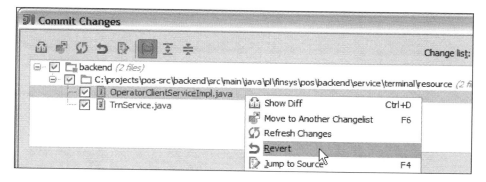

You will be presented with the **Revert** dialog box (shown in the following screenshot), where you can select one or more files you want to revert changes for:

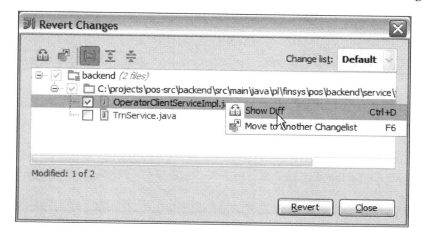

IntelliJ IDEA's UI design is very consistent, as with almost every file list related to version control. You can use the *Ctrl + D* (PC) or *cmd + D* (Mac) keyboard shortcut to see the differences.

You can also revert the file by picking **Revert** from the context menu available in the files tree in the **Project** tool window, as shown in the following screenshot:

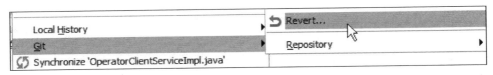

The same action can be executed from the **Changes** tool window. Select the file or the whole changelist and pick **Revert** from the context menu, as shown here:

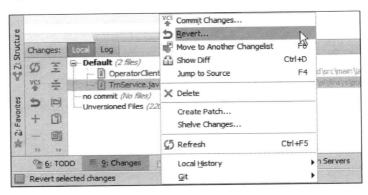

From the **Changes** view, you can also shelve the changes. To shelve, select the whole changelist or individual files and choose **Shelve** from the context menu. The **Shelve Changes** dialog box will show up with the selection you made.

When we work with the version control system, either by committing or updating the changes, we often need to see what the differences are. Let's take a look at how to work with the difference viewer now.

Using the difference viewer

The **Show Diff** command, available on the file or directory context menu, executes the difference viewer. This is the same tool we described in *Chapter 3, The Editor*, with one subtle difference. When it comes to the version control, it will compare your local version of the file with the revision taken from the version control.

The window contains your local revision of the file in the right pane and the revision you are comparing in the left pane. The modified lines will be highlighted in color.

Using the diff viewer, you can make changes to your local file. You can either copy the modified lines from the left (include changes) or delete your locally modified lines by using the icons in the gutter of the displayed files:

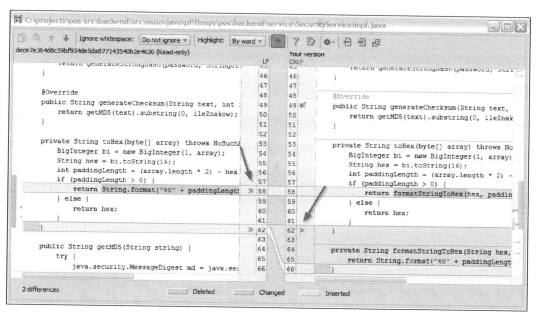

The number of differences is displayed in the status bar as shown in the following screenshot:

Clicking on the icons in the gutter will either copy (the arrow icons) or remove (the cross icon) the change. If you execute the difference viewer on the folder of the files (on the whole changelist, for example), you can switch to the next or previous file using the buttons on the toolbar or by using *Alt* + the left/right arrow keys:

To quickly go to the next or previous difference in the code, use the arrow button icons in the toolbar as shown here:

You can tweak the display of the diff viewer by amending options using the toolbar. For example, you can decide if you want to compare the whitespace characters, that have been highlight by word or line, toggle between displaying the whitespace or using line wraps. The differences viewer is very handy; you don't need an external tool to effectively compare files. The IDE gives you the possibility to see the differences between your local revision of the file and the same repository revision, another branch, or the latest repository revision. To compare with the specific revision, select the appropriate option from the file context menu:

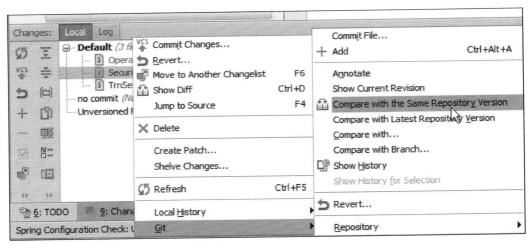

There is also a button in the main toolbar of IntelliJ that allows you to quickly show differences of the currently open (or selected, if you are in the project tree or in the changes view) file compared to the repository version:

The difference viewer is especially useful when it comes to browsing the history of the file. Let's look at the history now.

Displaying the history

When working with the version control, one of the most frequently used activities is looking at the file's timeline—what was changed in the past. To see the history of the file, select **Show history** from the file's context menu in the **Changes** tool window. It will be **Git** and then **Show History** in our example, as shown in the following screenshot:

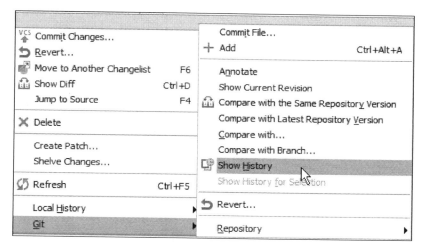

Again, you can use the button on the main toolbar to quickly access the history of the file as shown in the following screenshot:

IntelliJ IDEA will fetch the history log from the version control you are using and display the results in the **History** tab in the **Version Control** tool window. You will see the version number, the date of the commit, author, and commit message, as shown in the following screenshot:

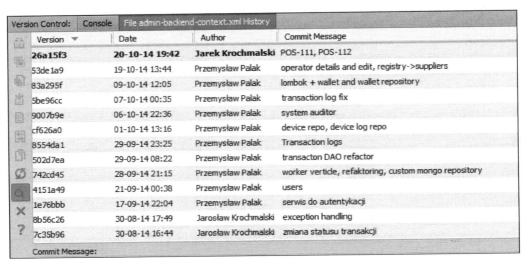

This is a lot of useful information but the best part is that you can now compare two versions of the file. Select the revisions you want to compare and use the *Ctrl + D* (PC) or *cmd + D* (Mac) keyboard shortcut or choose **Compare** from the context menu. Take note that if you compare two revisions fetched from the VCS, they will be read-only in the difference viewer:

The **History** browser is an invaluable tool to see what was changed in the past.

Yet another option to track the history of the versioned files is to turn the annotations on. If you want to see the VCS annotations in the editor itself, you can toggle annotations in the **VCS** menu. This will be **Git** and then the **Annotate** command, if you are using Git.

> A quick way to show annotations is to right-click on the left gutter area and select **Annotate** from the context menu that appears. This works for every VCS supported by IntelliJ IDEA.

The annotations panel will be appended to the editor, showing the commit number, the date of modification, and the author who modified the specific line in the source code, as shown in the following screenshot:

If you are using Git, apart from the history and annotations, IntelliJ IDEA gives you a very powerful feature that can come in handy: **Git Log**.

The log viewer

The Git log viewer is available as one of the tabs of the **Changes** tool window. It represents the Git log graph and allows you to browse all the changes that were made in the Git repository. It lets you list the project history, filter it, and search for specific changes. While Git's `status` command lets you inspect the working directory and staging area, **Log** only operates on the committed history. The main part of the Log view is the list of revisions. To quickly find a specific commit, just start typing its name in the search field. You can filter the list by branch, user, and date by using drop-down menus in the Log view toolbar. Select an item in the tree to see the list of files modified by the selected commit, as shown in the following screenshot:

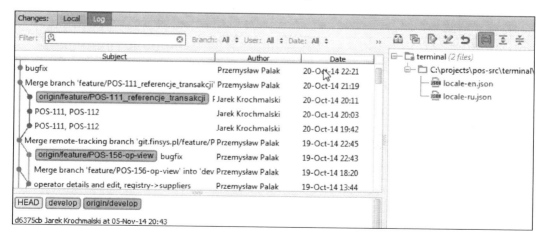

Every revision in the tree has the context menu available. From here, you can execute Git-specific commands on the selected commit such as **Cherry-pick**, for example:

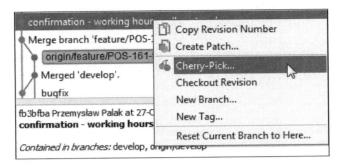

Of course, you can still use Git commands to display the log in the shell of your OS or in the **Terminal** tool window. This can be `git log --graph --all --decorate --oneline -boundary` for example. Using the **Log** viewer in IntelliJ IDEA is a lot more convenient.

> Basically, the Git log is a full featured Git GUI tool and doesn't require you to remember all of Git's command-line switches. And best of all, it's available out of the box in your IDE—you don't need to buy any external tool to work with your repository.

Now, you have an overview of how to work with version control actions in IntelliJ IDEA. Because you will use these commands often, the IDE introduces a quick way of running these commands.

Quickly executing VCS actions

Most of the version control commands can be executed quickly by using the **VCS Operations** pop up. Use the *Alt + '* (PC) or *control + V* (Mac) keyboard shortcut to see it:

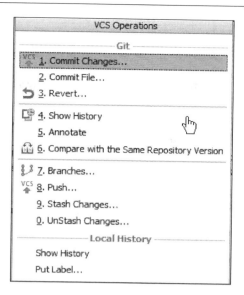

As you may remember from the previous chapters, you can use the powerful **Search Everywhere** action by clicking on the left shift twice:

Just start typing the VCS command you want to execute to quickly filter out the list. The **Search Everywhere** option is very good, but nothing beats a single keystroke. Let's summarize the shortcuts related to version control now.

Keyboard shortcuts

The following table summarizes the version control actions and associated shortcuts:

Action	PC shortcut	Mac shortcut
Commit project	*Ctrl + K*	*cmd + K*
Update project	*Ctrl + T*	*cmd + T*
View recent changes	*Alt + Shift + C*	*control + Shift + C*
VCS operations quick pop up	*Alt + '*	*control + V*

Summary

After reading this chapter, you know how to set up version control, get the project from the repository, commit your work, and get the changes made by other members of your team. Version control in IntelliJ IDEA is tightly integrated into the IDE. All the versioning activities can be executed from the IDE itself—you will not need to use an external tool for this. I believe it will shortly become natural for you to use the provided functionalities. Not being distracted by the use of external tools will result in higher effectiveness.

The last few chapters we focused on the IDE workspace itself, installing plugins, and using the editor, debugger, and version control. This should be enough to get you going. The IDE is very extensible; the list of available plugins is growing constantly. However, if this is not enough, you can create the plugin you need by using the provided plugin API. We will cover this in the next chapter.

10
Not Enough? Extend It

Apart from the core editor and debugger components provided by IDEA, most of the additional functionalities are available by using plugins. IDEA is modular in its nature. We already talked a lot about plugins in the previous chapters. If you want to write in a language other than Java, you need the corresponding plugins. If you require the IDE to support the framework of your choice, be it Spring or Vaadin, you need the plugin as well. The JetBrains team made a lot of additional plugins available in their repository. There are also a lot of plugins available from independent vendors; you can browse through them in **Settings**. The list of plugins is growing constantly. However, if you find it insufficient, let's say you want to incorporate some custom tool your company uses, IDEA provides a well-documented API helpful to develop your own extension. We will focus on writing one in this chapter. The whole plugin API is huge and it's surely out of the scope of this book. The plugin we will be creating will not be very sophisticated; it will just display the famous "Hello world" message, but the chapter should give you an overview of how to create your own extension and will maybe inspire you to create something great you will want to share with the community.

We will cover the following topics in this chapter:

- Setting up the environment and creating a plugin project
- Developing plugin functionality
- Testing, deploying, and publishing

Setting up the environment and project

To work on your own plugin, you can use either the Community or the Ultimate Edition of IntelliJ IDEA; both these editions are well-suited to plugin development. To be able to debug IDEA's core code though, you will need to use the Community Edition and have the Community Edition sources available on the source path of the plugin project. It's not mandatory for the plugin development process but can sometimes be useful. To get the Community Edition source, we need to pull it out from the repository; it's open source. Take note that the size of the sources will be more than one gigabyte, so make sure you have plenty of free space on your drive.

To pull out the source from the repository, use the Git `pull` command in the shell of your operating system:

```
git clone git://git.jetbrains.org/idea/community.git idea
```

 You can use the `--depth 1` Git option to create a shallow Git clone. This will speed up the download process; the history will be truncated to a depth of one. Note that this will be useful if you develop a plugin against the current version of IDEA released. In all other cases, you have to check out the tag/branch for a specific version of IDEA that you are working on in order to be sure that you are using the right APIs.

The pulling process will take a while, depending on the speed of your Internet connection. While waiting, you can switch to your IDEA instance and make sure the plugin named **Plugin DevKit** is enabled; you will need it later to run and debug your own plugin.

 If your plugin is going to have additional windows, dialog boxes, or other UI components, you may find the UI Designer plugin helpful as well; make sure it's enabled in the **Plugins** section in **Settings**.

We now have the Community Edition code retrieved and the necessary plugins installed. Let's create the plugin project.

The plugin project is very similar to an ordinary Java project, with some subtle differences. Refer to *Chapter 2, Off We Go – To the Code* for an overview of how to create a new project.

To start developing the plugin, create a new project of type **IntelliJ Platform Plugin**. You will need to set up IDEA's own SDK for the project; click on **New** and then point to the installation of your IDE. The correct path will be filled in automatically, as shown in the following screenshot:

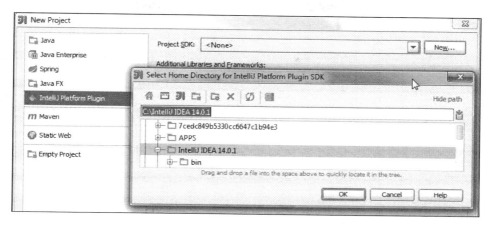

Click on **OK** and then select the required SDK version from the drop-down list. Proceed with the project wizard and provide a name for your plugin project and its location, as shown here:

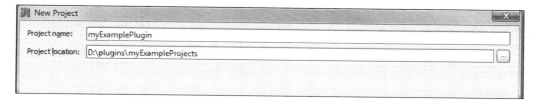

If you click on **Finish**, IDEA will create the project with one single module. When done, your project structure should look like the following screenshot:

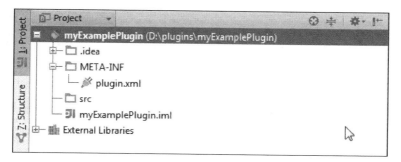

Note that the plugin modules have a nice plug icon attached to easily distinguish them from other module types, as shown in the following screenshot. Note that the run/debug configuration will also be created for you automatically with the proper VM settings.

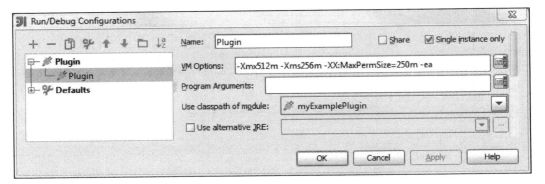

Starting a run/debug configuration for the plugin will spawn the second IntelliJ IDEA instance. If you encounter freezes when starting your plugin in development mode (most frequently, those are crashes during index rebuilding), you may want to adjust these VM settings.

Alternatively, you can start developing plugins by creating an ordinary, plain Java project, but this is not very convenient. In this case, you will need to manually create a single module of type **IntelliJ Platform Plugin** and attach **IntelliJ Platform Plugin SDK** to it. Also, the run/debug configuration needs to be created by hand.

If you want to be able to debug core classes of the IDE itself, you will need to include the sources of the Community Edition you pulled out from the repository earlier. To do this, open the **Project Structure** dialog box, switch to the **Platform** settings, and choose the SDK you created as **IntelliJ Platform Plugin SDK** earlier. In the **Project Structure** dialog box, switch to the **Sourcepath** tab and include the downloaded source directory using the *Alt + Insert* keyboard shortcut, as shown in the following screenshot:

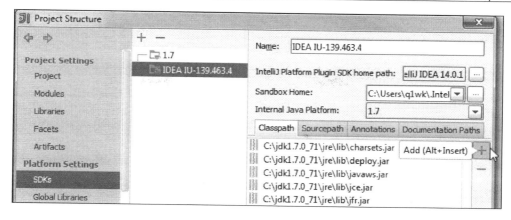

IntelliJ IDEA will then scan for source roots and begin to index recently included sources; this will take a while. Our development setup is now ready. We can start developing the plugin functionality now.

Developing the plugin functionality

When it comes to plugin development, IntelliJ IDEA introduces the concept of the component. There can be components at the application, module, and project level. Application level (global) components are initialized when the IDE starts. Project level components, on the other hand, are instantiated by the IDE for every project instance opened. Module level components, accordingly, are instantiated for every project's module loaded.

A further concept introduced in the plugins API is *action*. Here, action represents the toolbar or menu item. It's a class whose `actionPerformed` method is called when the toolbar button or menu item is selected. Action can be either defined in the configuration file, or instantiated and registered programmatically. Every single action must have a unique identifier.

IntelliJ IDEA provides the mechanism of groups to group actions; a group represents the menu or toolbar. The IDE itself has its own groups defined. By adding your actions to the already defined groups, your plugin can present its own items in the IDE's standard menus and toolbars. Groups can contain other groups as well.

If a plugin will interact with other plugins or with the IntelliJ IDEA core, it must declare one or more extension points and extensions. Think about an Extension Point as a socket that something else can plug into. The extension on the other hand is like a plug you can connect into the Extension Point. Each Extension Point defines a class or an interface that is allowed to plug into it. The IDE itself contains a lot of Extension Points defined to allow you to plug in and extend the core functionality.

If you would like to reuse the common functionality between your components or just delegate some behavior to the external class, you can use the concept of services. A service is a plugin component loaded on demand when your component or action calls for it. A service is a singleton; it will be instantiated only once during the first call. You call a service by executing the static getService () method on the ServiceManager object. The services, just like components, have three scopes: application, project, and module. We will create a simple service later in this chapter.

All the Components, Extension Points, Services, Action, and Groups must be defined in the plugin configuration file, plugin.xml. This file describes the features and the contents of a plugin. Think about it as a plugin deployment descriptor—the IDE will analyze the file, instantiate all the necessary classes, and make necessary hooks to make the plugin work.

Let's summarize the concepts now:

The concept	The functionality
Application component	Created and initialized on IntelliJ IDEA startup
Project component	Created for each project instance
Module component	Created for each module in every project loaded
Extension point	Allow other plugins to extend this plugin functionality
Extension	Allow this plugin to extend the core IntelliJ IDEA or other plugin functionality
Service	The singleton loaded on demand available for other plugins' components
Action	The class whose actionPerformed method is called when the menu item or toolbar button is selected
Group	A group of actions form a toolbar or menu
Configuration file	The plugin.xml file with all the definitions of Components, Services, Actions, and Groups with references to their implementations

Our plugin should display a new menu item; clicking on this will show the message on the screen. As you may have guessed, for the purpose of our example, we will use Action. To make the example more illustrative, the message to display will come from the service.

The easiest way to create plugin modules is to use the provided wizards. The list of wizards is available in the context menu. Right-click on the **src** directory of the plugin module and choose **New**, and then **Action**, as shown in the following screenshot:

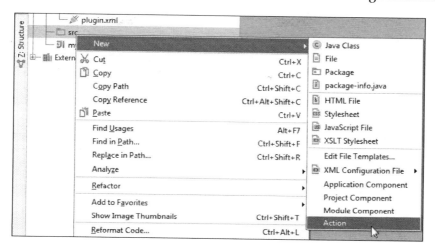

The **New Action** wizard will pop up, asking for a new ID for the action, its **Name** that will identify the new action in the UI, and the name of the class with the action's implementation. In the **Groups** list, we select the Group that represents the main menu, and in the **Actions** list, we select the **WindowMenu** action. The **Anchor** option defines the order in which we would like to include our action within the selected group: **First**, **Last**, **Before**, and **After**. Let's choose **After** to have our menu placed after the **Window** menu, as shown in the following screenshot:

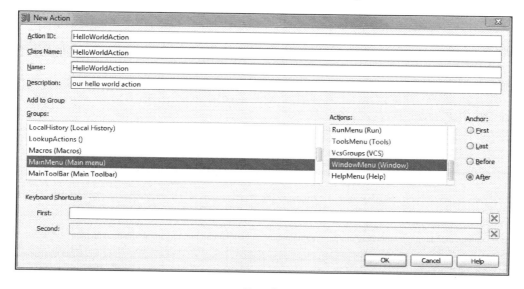

If you click on **OK**, IntelliJ IDEA will generate the `HelloWorldAction` class skeleton and place the reference to it in the `plugin.xml` file. The `plugin.xml` file contains the details of the plugin such as its name and description, vendor information, and the applicable IDE version number. For our case, the most interesting part of this file is a list of all the actions and components with references to their implementation classes. In our example, it will be just a single `Action` element with the `class` attribute set to the `HelloWorldAction` and `add-to-group` element attaching it to the main menu, or, to be precise, to the group with the ID `MainMenu`. The autogenerated code looks like the following screenshot:

```
<actions>
    <!-- Add your actions here -->
    <action id="HelloWorldAction" class="HelloWorldAction" text="HelloWorldAction"
            description="our hello world action"
            icon="icons/smiley.png">
        <add-to-group group-id="MainMenu" anchor="after" relative-to-action="WindowMenu"/>
    </action>
</actions>
```

The names of the elements and attributes in the `plugin.xml` file are rather self-explanatory. The generated comments will get you started fast. There are `<application-components>` and `<project-components>` elements where you can put the references to your own components. The actions are enclosed in the `<actions>` element. The internal, existing IDE actions identifiers can be found in the `IdeActions` interface. Navigate to this interface by using the **Go To Class** keyboard shortcut: *Ctrl + N* (PC) or *cmd + O* (Mac).

The services should be defined with the `<applicationService>`, `<projectService>`, or `<moduleService>` element placed inside the `<extensions>` element. To define extensions and points of an extension, place them within the `<extensions>` and `<extensionPoints>` elements accordingly.

IntelliJ IDEA will provide you with the code completion when editing the `plugin.xml` file. As you will remember from the previous chapters, *Ctrl + Space Bar* will execute the code completion pop up; in this case, suggesting the names of the XML elements and predefined values, as shown in the following screenshot:

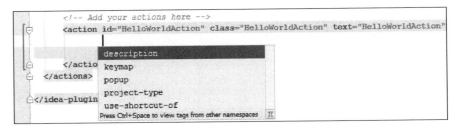

If you make a mistake in the plugin definition file, IntelliJ IDEA will give you the error message when you try to run your configuration, as shown in the following screenshot. The error description may be useful to quickly find out where the problem is.

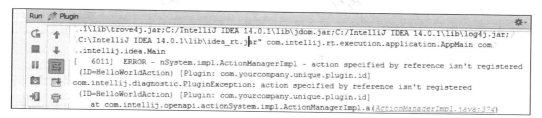

Let's change some of the generated code. It would be good to have a nice icon for our action; we need to add the `icon` attribute pointing to the bitmap image in the source path. In our example, we will use an 18 x 18 pixel PNG file. Additionally, we will create our own new group and attach it to the main menu and the main IntelliJ IDEA's toolbar. The group will contain the reference to our action. To create the reference, we will use the `reference` element. The service providing the message to be displayed will be defined in the `<extensions>` element as the `<applicationService>` element. The modified code fragment will look like the following screenshot:

```xml
<extensions defaultExtensionNs="com.intellij">
    <!-- Add your extensions here -->
    <applicationService serviceInterface="DayOfWeekService" serviceImplementation="DayOfWeekServiceImpl"/>
</extensions>

<actions>
    <!-- Add your actions here -->
    <action id="HelloWorldAction" class="HelloWorldAction" text="IntelliJ IDEA Essentials"
            icon="icons/smiley.png">
    </action>
    <group id="ourSampleGroup" text="our plugin menu" description="Our new group">
        <reference ref="HelloWorldAction"/>
        <add-to-group group-id="MainMenu" anchor="after" relative-to-action="WindowMenu"/>
        <add-to-group group-id="MainToolBar" anchor="after" relative-to-action="HelpTopics"/>
    </group>
</actions>
```

If you select the **New Action** or **New Component** dialog box again later, the IDE will add new references to the existing `plugin.xml` file.

The main functionality of the action is contained in the implementation class. When the newly created Platform Plugin SDK is first used, IntelliJ IDEA will prompt to attach its annotations to the platform SDK:

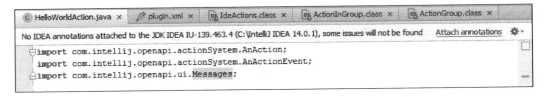

Attaching the annotations will create a lot of hints and inspections related to the plugin development available in the editor, so attaching these annotations is a no-brainer.

The auto generated code is just a skeleton; the body of the `actionPerformed` method is empty, so our action does nothing. Let's make it do something useful, for example, let's show the message with the current day of the week. Change the `actionPerformed` method to something like the following screenshot:

```java
public class HelloWorldAction extends AnAction {
    public void actionPerformed(AnActionEvent e) {
        DayOfWeekService dayOfWeekService = ServiceManager.getService(DayOfWeekService.class);

        System.out.println("Hello world action performed!");
        Messages.showMessageDialog(dayOfWeekService.getDayOfWeek(), "Information",
            Messages.getInformationIcon());
    }
}
```

Of course, we need the service interface and its implementation. Note that our service needs to implement the `ApplicationComponent` interface with life cycle methods such as `initComponent` and `disposeComponent`. The following screenshot shows our service's interface:

```java
public interface DayOfWeekService {
    public String getDayOfWeek();
}
```

The code's implementation is shown as follows:

```java
import com.intellij.openapi.components.ApplicationComponent;
import org.jetbrains.annotations.NotNull;

import java.text.SimpleDateFormat;
import java.util.Date;

public class DayOfWeekServiceImpl implements DayOfWeekService, ApplicationComponent {

    public String getDayOfWeek() {
        SimpleDateFormat simpleDateFormat = new SimpleDateFormat("EEEE");
        return String.format("Hello, World! It's %s", simpleDateFormat.format(new Date()));
    }

    @Override
    public void initComponent() {

    }

    @Override
    public void disposeComponent() {

    }

    @NotNull
    @Override
    public String getComponentName() {
        return "DayFinder";
    }
}
```

After adding the required Java imports, believe it or not, our plugin is ready to be tested. Let's run it.

Deploying and publishing

If you created the project as an **IDEA Platform Plugin** project, the proper run/debug configuration should already be present in the **Run/Debug Configurations** drop down. Otherwise, if you decided to start from the Java project, you will need to define the run/debug configuration on your own. Refer to the *Running your project* section of *Chapter 5, Make It Happen – Running Your Project*, for information on how to create a runtime or debug configuration.

When developing plugins, the required profile type is **Plugin**, as shown here:

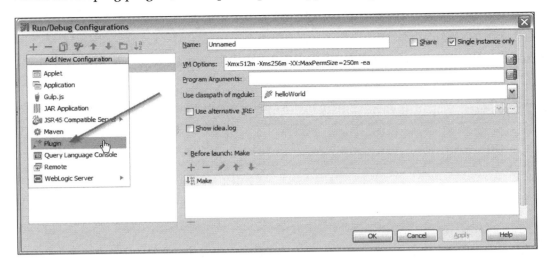

Running or debugging a configuration profile defined in this way will spawn a second instance of IntelliJ.

When running the plugin development run/debug configuration for the first time, a completely new instance of IntelliJ IDEA will be started, complete with its own set of settings. A few dialog boxes will pop up asking you to import settings or enter your license. Don't worry, it will not overwrite your *base* IntelliJ IDEA installation settings.

Our plugin will be installed automatically. This is the moment when having a source of the Community Edition on the source path comes in handy; you can debug IntelliJ IDEA's own source code if something goes wrong.

Our day name reminder plugin will be active and the new action can be seen in the toolbar (or, in other words, in the group with `group-id MainToolBar`), as shown in the following screenshot:

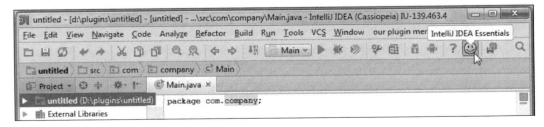

Of course, in the menu (again, contained in the subgroup of the group with the group-id MainMenu value) the clicking action will execute the actionPerformed method, as shown in the following screenshot:

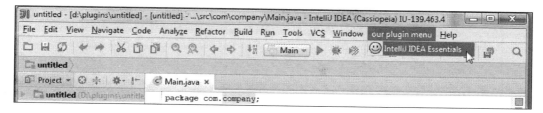

Next, the name of the current day will pop up on the screen as shown here, notifying you of the good news:

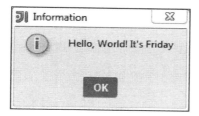

Take note that all of the log output from the second instance of the IntelliJ IDEA goes to the log pane in the **Run** tool window, as shown here; you can use this for your own purposes too:

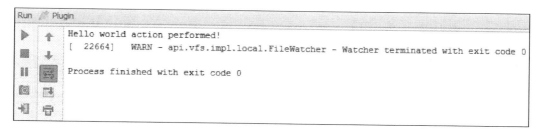

Our plugin works flawlessly, so it's time to release it to the world. To do this, we will need to deploy it. To prepare the deployment package, execute **Prepare All Plugin Modules For Deployment** from the **Build** menu, as shown in the following screenshot:

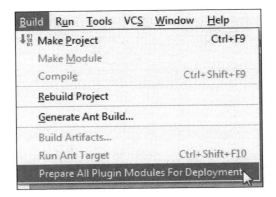

After a while, IntelliJ IDEA will create a distributable .jar file and notify you about its location and it'll display a notification as shown here:

The archive file will contain all the compiled classes with our implementation and the META-INF directory with the plugin description file, plugin.xml. Now it's ready to be distributed. You are now the plugin author, so you should have the JetBrains account. You can register the account at the JetBrains Account Center web page at http://account.jetbrains.com. If you're ready, visit https://plugins.jetbrains.com, log in with your credentials, and click on the **Add new plugin** button. After uploading the archive, the plugin will be submitted for moderation by the JetBrains team. The process will take a couple of days. In the meanwhile, you can provide some additional info, such as the license type, bug tracker and forum URL, and other information that should be included on the plugin's site or when browsing the plugin list in the **Plugins** section of **Settings** in the IDE.

Summary

Writing our own plugins in IntelliJ IDEA is not as tricky as it may seem; it's all about the API provided by the JetBrains team, basically. This chapter covers just the beginning of plugin development for IntelliJ IDEA. It is just the tip of the iceberg. You can find the documentation of the API by heading to JetBrains' Confluence page and choosing the IntelliJ IDEA plugin development space. At the time of writing this book, the documentation was available at:

```
http://confluence.jetbrains.com/display/IDEADEV/PluginDevelopment
```

Here, you will find the IDE's architectural overview, the plugin structure, and many guides on how to develop even the most advanced plugins. JetBrains Confluence is the never-ending resource to extend the IDE. The explanation of IntelliJ IDEA's virtual file system, development of the version control, and custom language plugins is all here. The FAQ section with a lot of interesting questions already answered can be supportive too.

 The JetBrains DevNet forums are of great help if the information cannot be found in Confluence. The forum can be found at `https://www.jetbrains.com/devnet/idea/`.

In the Sample Plugins section, you will find the source code and description of how to create plugins of different types. A few other good sources when preparing for your journey of plugin development are:

- Blogs of authors of other plugins
- The source code of IntelliJ open source plugins
- The source code of open source projects created by other users

After reading the tutorials, browsing through the API, and reading source codes, only your imagination will be the limit when it comes to extending the IDE.

Index

A

action 242
application component 242
artifacts 35-37

B

breakpoints
  deleting 181
  Field Watchpoint, creating 183
  filtering 187
  managing 180-191
  method breakpoint 180

C

changelists, version control 217, 218
Change Signature refactoring 100
changes, version control
  browsing 226, 227
  getting, from repository 224-226
  local changes, reverting 227, 228
clipboard history, editor 70
code, editor
  completing 71, 72
  creating 74
  inspecting 75, 76
  reformatting 70
Colors and Fonts, IDE 18, 19
color themes
  URL 19
column selection mode, editor 69

configuration

defaults 134
permanent configuration 121, 122
sharing 135
temporary configuration 120, 121
configuration file 242
configuration profile
  debugging 248-250
  running 248-250
Convert Anonymous Class to Inner
  refactoring 114
Convert to Instance Method refactoring 101
Copy refactoring 96

D

debug configuration
  creating, for test 160-164
  for Java application 122-127
  running 136, 137
debugger
  actions 203-205
  keyboard shortcuts 206
  options 172-174
  settings 171-176
  starting 191, 192
debugging 171
Debug tool window
  about 193-196
  Frames tab 194, 195
  Threads tab 194, 195
Delegate refactoring 107, 108
deployment, plugin 247
difference viewer, version control
  using 228-231

directory-based format

about 44

versus file-based format 45

docked mode 11

don't repeat yourself (DRY) principle 96

E

Eclipse

and IntelliJ IDEA 27

editions

comparing 7, 8

editor

about 47

gutter area 48-51

scratches 55

scrollbar 56, 57

status bar 51-53

tabs 53, 54

editor, basics

about 67

clipboard history 70

code, completing 71, 72

code, generating 74

code, inspecting 75, 76

code, reformatting 70, 71

column selection mode 69

language injection 73, 74

syntax-aware selection 69

text, replacing 67, 68

text, searching 67-69

editor tabs 16

Encapsulate Fields refactoring 115

Enterprise ARchive (EAR) 35

environment

setting up 238-241

Excluded folder 30

expressions

evaluating 196-203

extension 242

extension point 242

external documentation

viewing 86, 87

Extract Constant refactoring 102, 103

Extract Field refactoring 103

Extract Interface refactoring 109

Extract Method object refactoring 106

Extract method refactoring 105

Extract Parameter refactoring 104

Extract refactorings 102

Extract Superclass refactoring 110

Extract Variable refactoring 102

F

facets 33-35

Field Watchpoint

creating 183, 184

defining 190

file-based format

about 44

versus directory-based format 45

files

adding, to version control 218-220

committing 220-224

comparing 80, 81

file switching actions 64

Find and Replace Code Duplicates
refactoring 96

floating mode 12

folders

comparing 82, 83

Excluded 30

Resources 30

Sources 29

Test Resources 30

Tests 29

G

Generify refactoring 116, 117

Global (IDE) level, libraries 31

Gradle

tasks, executing 150, 151

URL 139

using 148-150

group 242

gutter area, editor 48-50

H

help

looking for 83

history, version control

displaying 231-233

Hotswap page 177

I

IDE, settings
  Colors and Fonts 18, 19
  keyboard shortcuts 17, 18
  options, searching for 17
  plugins, picking 19, 20
inline documentation
  viewing 84
Inline refactoring 110, 111
IntelliJ IDEA
  editions, comparing 7, 8
  installing 8, 9
  tuning 23, 24
Introduce Parameter Object refactoring 105
Invert Boolean refactoring 113

J

Java application
  debug configuration 122-128
  run configuration 122-128
JavaScript debugger
  setting up 178, 179
JetBrains
  URL 7, 8
JetBrains Account Center
  URL 250
JetBrains DevNet forums
  URL 251
Just-In-Time (JIT) compiler 181

K

keyboard shortcuts, debugger 206
keyboard shortcuts, IDE
  setting 17, 18
keyboard shortcuts, refactoring 117
keyboard shortcuts, test 170
keyboard shortcuts, version control
  actions, executing 236

L

language injection 73
libraries
  about 31
  Global (IDE) level 31

  module level 31
  project level 31
Live Templates
  about 76-78
  postfix code completion 79, 80
log viewer, version control 233, 234

M

Make Static refactoring 101
Maven
  goals, running 144-148
  settings, editing 140-143
  URL 139
Maven tool window 144
method breakpoint 180
method parameters
  viewing 85
module component 242
module level, libraries 31
modules 28, 29
Move Instance Method refactoring 99
Move refactoring 97, 98

N

navigating
  between files 58-64
  in editor 57
  within single file 64-66
NetBeans
  and IntelliJ IDEA 27
Node.js configuration 133, 134

O

options
  searching for 17

P

permanent configuration
  about 121, 122
  Node.js configuration 133, 134
  run/debug configuration, for Java
    application 123-128
  Tomcat server local configuration,
    creating 128-132

pinned mode 11
plugin
  deployment 247
  functionality, developing 241-247
  picking 19, 20
  publishing 247
postfix code completion 79, 80
project
  about 26
  artifacts 36, 37
  checking out, from repository 209, 210
  configuration 26
  facets 33-35
  folders 29-31
  libraries 31-33
  modules 28, 29
  setting up 238-240
  structure 26
project component 242
project, creating
  about 37
  existing project, importing 40-43
  format 43
  from scratch 38-40
project, format
  directory-based format 44
  directory-based format,
      versus file-based format 45
  file-based format 44
project level, libraries 31
publishing, plugin 247
Pull Members Up refactoring 113
Push Members Down refactoring 113

R

refactoring
  keyboard shortcuts 117
  overview 89-94
  URL 89
refactoring actions
  about 95
  Change Signature 100
  Convert Anonymous Class to Inner 114
  Convert to Instance Method 101

Copy 96
Delegate 107, 108
Encapsulate Fields 115
Extract Constant 102, 103
Extract Field 103
Extract Interface 109
Extract method 105
Extract Method object 106
Extract Parameter 104
Extract refactorings 102
Extract Superclass 110
Extract Variable 102
Find and Replace Code Duplicates 96
Generify 116, 117
Inline 110, 111
Introduce Parameter Object 105
Invert Boolean 113
Make Static 101
Move 97, 98
Move Instance Method 99
Pull Members Up 113
Push Members Down 113
Remove Middleman 112
Rename 95
Replace Constructor with Builder 116
Replace Constructor with Factory
    Method 116
Replace Inheritance With Delegation 113
Safe Delete 99
Type Migration 101
Wrap Return Value 112
Remove Middleman refactoring 112
Rename refactoring 95
Replace Constructor with Builder
    refactoring 116
Replace Constructor with Factory Method
    refactoring 116
Replace Inheritance With Delegation
    refactoring 113
repository
  project, checking out from 209, 210
Resources folder 30
run configuration
  creating, for test 160-164
  for Java application 122-128
  running 136, 137

S

Safe Delete refactoring 99
scratches, editor 55
scrollbar, editor 56, 57
Search Everywhere feature 66, 67
service 242
settings
  exporting 21
  importing 21
  sharing 22, 23
SOLID principles
  URL 107
Sources folder 29
split mode 12
status bar, editor 51-53
Subversion (SVN) 208
syntax-aware selection, editor 69

T

tabs, editor 53, 54
temporary configuration 120, 121
test
  creating 156-160
  debug configuration, creating 160-164
  debugging 164-169
  keyboard shortcuts 170
  run configuration, creating 160-164
  running 164-169
testing plugins
  enabling 154, 155
Test Resources folder 30
Tests folder 29
text
  replacing 68, 69
  searching 67, 68
themes
  URL 22
Tomcat server local configuration
  creating 128-132
tool windows
  about 9, 10
  multiple views 13, 14

navigating inside 14
view modes 11
tool windows, multiple views
  about 13, 14
  navigating inside 14
  setting up, for specific project 15, 16
tool windows, view modes
  docked mode 11
  floating mode 12
  pinned mode 11
  split mode 12
type definition
  viewing 84
Type Migration refactoring 101

U

Ultimate Edition
  commercial license 8
  personal license 8
usages
  looking for 85

V

variables
  inspecting 196-203
version control
  about 207
  actions, executing 234, 235
  changelists 217, 218
  changes, browsing 226, 227
  changes, obtaining from repository 224-226
  configuring 210-217
  difference viewer, using 228-230
  enabling 207, 208
  files, adding 218-220
  files, committing 220-224
  history, displaying 231-233
  local changes, reverting 227, 228
  log viewer 233, 234
Version Control System
        (VCS) *See* version control

W

workspace
  about 9
  editor tabs 16
  tool windows 9, 10
  tool windows, multiple views 13, 14
  tool windows, view modes 11
Wrap Return Value refactoring 112

Thank you for buying
IntelliJ IDEA Essentials

About Packt Publishing

Packt, pronounced 'packed', published its first book, *Mastering phpMyAdmin for Effective MySQL Management*, in April 2004, and subsequently continued to specialize in publishing highly focused books on specific technologies and solutions.

Our books and publications share the experiences of your fellow IT professionals in adapting and customizing today's systems, applications, and frameworks. Our solution-based books give you the knowledge and power to customize the software and technologies you're using to get the job done. Packt books are more specific and less general than the IT books you have seen in the past. Our unique business model allows us to bring you more focused information, giving you more of what you need to know, and less of what you don't.

Packt is a modern yet unique publishing company that focuses on producing quality, cutting-edge books for communities of developers, administrators, and newbies alike. For more information, please visit our website at www.packtpub.com.

Writing for Packt

We welcome all inquiries from people who are interested in authoring. Book proposals should be sent to author@packtpub.com. If your book idea is still at an early stage and you would like to discuss it first before writing a formal book proposal, then please contact us; one of our commissioning editors will get in touch with you.

We're not just looking for published authors; if you have strong technical skills but no writing experience, our experienced editors can help you develop a writing career, or simply get some additional reward for your expertise.

Getting started with IntelliJ IDEA

ISBN: 978-1-84969-961-7   Paperback: 114 pages

Exploit IntelliJ IDEA's unique features to rapidly
develop web and Java Enterprise applications

1. Exhibit techniques that improve
    development performance.

2. Present framework support.

3. Create an application that explores the
    features of the integrated development
    environment (IDE).

Chef Essentials

ISBN: 978-1-78398-304-9   Paperback: 218 pages

Discover how to deploy software, manage hosts,
and scale your infrastructure with Chef

1. Learn how to use Chef in a concise manner.

2. Learn ways to use Chef to integrate with cloud
    services such as EC2 and Rackspace Cloud.

3. See advanced ways to integrate Chef into your
    environment, develop tests, and even extend
    Chef's core functionality.

Please check **www.PacktPub.com** for information on our titles

JavaScript Promises Essentials

ISBN: 978-1-78398-564-7   Paperback: 90 pages

Build fully functional web applications using Promises, the new standard in JavaScript

1. Integrate JavaScript Promises into your application by mastering the key concepts of the Promises API.

2. Replace complex nested callbacks in JavaScript with the more intuitive chained Promises.

3. Acquire the knowledge needed to start working with JavaScript Promises immediately.

Mockito Essentials

ISBN: 978-1-78398-360-5   Paperback: 214 pages

A practical guide to get you up and running with unit testing using Mockito

1. Explore Mockito features and learn stubbing, mocking and spying dependencies using the Mockito framework.

2. Mock external dependencies for legacy and greenfield projects and create an automated JUnit safety net for building reliable, maintainable, and testable software.

3. A focused guide filled with examples and supporting illustrations on testing your software using Mockito.

Please check **www.PacktPub.com** for information on our titles

64620404R00154

Made in the USA
Lexington, KY
19 June 2017